LAUNCHING AFTER LOCKDOWN

This book is dedicated to our wonderful grown-up family and their children, who are such a blessing.

LAUNCHING AFTER LOCKDOWN

Bob and Mary Bain

Open Wells Publishing

Shilbottle, Northumberland, United Kingdom
Bob and Mary Bain
e-mail; bobbain@hotmail.co.uk

CONTENTS

'Launching after Lockdown' is aptly illustrated by the cover photograph. We are taking off from the runway and are safe. Behind us, spectacular things are happening which we have had something to do with! What will your launch after lockdown look like?

In appreciation of:-

All those who have brought their experience, wisdom and friendship into our lives, especially our family.

Amongst them we would like to especially thank
Hugh Osgood and Gary Seithel for their pioneering example and inspiration.

Esther Heron and Flora Allenby who edited the text.

The <u>Welcome Network team</u>:-
Alicia and Gabriel Osinibi, Christen Forster, Michael Osinibi, Freda Brobby, Vikki Harrison, Steve and Gemma Carder, Ann Franklin, and all our supporters.

Our friends in Churches in Communities International, the Inter Prophetic and Apostolic Alliance, and the Network with no name yet!

<u>In Northumberland and Tyneside</u>:-
Alan Dickinson, Andy Raine, Robert Ward, Paul Merton, Pauline Fellows, Neil and Joan Sayers,
Jonathan and Jenny Mackwell,
and Peter and Theodora Adegbie.

Also our thanks to
<u>the Prayer Net team</u>:-Sandra Stuart, Carol Charlton, Joan Gladders, Fay Renwick, Aaron Shah and Steve Gill, and the <u>Open Wells planning team</u>:- Lynne and Doug Gowland, and Andrew and Michelle Duff.

Last but not least- <u>for our friends in Shilbottle,</u>
the church, and those who serve through the local Parish council and other community organizations.

PREFACE
A FAIRY TALE

The lockdown period in the UK has felt surreal to me, like a fairy tale, almost. We have been centre-stage in a story that hasn't finished yet, with its serious impact still being worked out over the whole earth. On a personal level, maybe we can find parallels in what we have experienced in a well-known fairy tale. I have chosen Goldilocks and the three bears, and I am letting you make the connections!

A STRANGE NEW ENVIRONMENT

Goldilocks arrived at the home of the three bears in the middle of the forest. She had no idea where she was, and had walked a long way. Initially there had been the excitement of an adventure in the forest. There had been all the fun of exploring. This was a strange new environment for her and there was a surreal quality about it. She had never really been in the forest properly before. It felt quite timeless as if the day would go on forever. Normal life back in the village was like a distant memory.

HOW LONG IS THIS GOING ON?

But where had the paths gone? The one she had been following had petered out. She sensed too that she was miles away from home, and what direction was home in anyhow? Could she ever find her way back? Would she experience normal life ever again? She began to wonder if she would be in the forest forever. Fear started to creep up and then grabbed hold of her. The forest didn't look such an exciting place now, and it wasn't dark yet! Right now, however, the sun was still shining through the trees, so she kept on going despite feeling very tired and hungry. She had eaten all her supply of snacks that she had piled in her bag when she'd left home earlier. She had also put in the bag things which she had thought were sensible at the time – some loo roll for example. But why two lots? How silly of her!

REDISCOVERING HOME

You can imagine her joy at seeing the home of the three bears just ahead of her. The little cottage looked so sweet and normal in the clearing! Inside, the kitchen was warm and cosy and how welcome the food looked! There were three bowls on the table, each one containing porridge. She decided it would be ok to have some. There was no-one there that she could ask. The house was so quiet and still but in a friendly sort of way. Goldilocks tasted the porridge from each of the bowls. To her surprise, the porridge in the first two larger bowls didn't really taste as good as she'd expected. The temperature was all wrong; but when she tried the porridge in the smallest bowl, it was a different story. It turned out to be just right for her!

LIFE BUT NOT AS WE KNOW IT

We won't carry on this story into what happened next, when the three bears returned home to find Goldilocks asleep. We will leave her still eating the porridge and return to our own real lives. Except our life at this time doesn't feel like real life, as we were used to knowing it! An element of the surreal is all about us. We still seem to be in some kind of a fairy tale! The range of emotions we have experienced over recent months in this strange new environment of lockdown has included excitement and fear, and also just plain weariness. We have stocked up our food cupboard as best as our funds would allow, watched the news and kept two metres apart from everyone else. We have wondered where this story is all going. It has felt odd, very odd!

FEELING ALONE

In the story, Goldilocks is alone. She is alone in the forest and alone in the cottage of the three bears. This isn't true of real life. We may feel alone but there really is a God in Heaven, who made us and who cares for us. Goldilocks was making decisions by herself, but we have the amazing reassurance that God is with us, whatever we are experiencing, and can help us come through this very different period which is upon us. God is the one who can steady our emotions and bring us to a place of peace. He can be left out of a fairy tale, but He mustn't be left out of our understanding of real life.

TASTE AND SEE

Like Goldilocks eating the porridge in the smallest bowl, what's on offer in this small book about launching out after lockdown, may taste just right for you. I don't know what you have been through in this strange period, but God does. He knows each one of us and is with us in every phase and circumstance of our lives. Regarding this book, there is only one way to find out if it is just right for you. Pick up the spoon and eat. These words from the Psalms seem very appropriate, whatever you are feeling about life at this time, *'Taste and see that the Lord is good'* (Ps.34:8).

And if it is all seeming too much, Jesus says in Matthew's gospel, *'Come to me all you who are weary and burdened, and I will give you rest. Take my yoke upon you and learn from me for I am gentle and humble in heart and you will find rest for your souls.'* (Matthew 11:28-29). Thankfully God is not a fairy tale but our very present help in times of trouble (Psalm 46:1). He really is here to help us as we launch out after lockdown.

PART ONE
GOD IS WITH US

CHAPTER ONE
AN UPPER ROOM
LOCKDOWN

Jesus brings peace to our fears and is with us. Our faith in him is fact-based, supported by the first hand witness accounts of his resurrection.

NORMAL LIFE HAD STOPPED

It was in the build-up to Easter, as I prepared an online Sunday message for a group of churches in my home region of Northumberland, that I began to see, and be amazed by, the parallels between what we have been going through in this pandemic, and the experience of the first followers of Jesus, just a few days after His death. The resurrection had happened but they hadn't really understood what it all meant yet. Their main feelings were that everything that had become normal life for them over three and half years of being with Jesus, had suddenly ground to a halt. They had walked and ate, adventured, and lived their lives with Jesus throughout that time, and now he had been brutally taken from them. Suddenly everything had changed – there was a sense of loss and also a very present feeling of danger too. Just like Jesus, they also might be grabbed hold of by the authorities, and suffer a gruesome death at their hands.

FEAR LOCKS US IN

In John's gospel, chapter twenty, we can read about the way the disciples reacted to their sudden change of circumstances and the threat that they now faced. Their knee-jerk reaction was absolute fear. All former courage and brave posturing had instantly vanished from them, and basic survival mode had kicked in. They rushed inside, closed the doors, and locked themselves in - *'for fear of the Jews'* (John 20:19). This has been our situation too. There has been a very real threat from Covid-19 in this pandemic. Our knee-jerk reaction has been to lockdown and isolate in order to minimise the danger of death. Sensible survival measures have been implemented, sometimes painfully slowly, but there has also been a lot of fear. As we have heard the stories of what has happened to others, and the daily death numbers, nationally and globally, fear has gripped our communities.

JESUS IS HERE

For the first disciples of Jesus, locked away in an upper room, the presence of Jesus, suddenly standing among them, was a big shock. They hadn't taken in the promise which he'd made to them of His resurrection. He'd said he would be back, raised from the dead, but none of their plans had factored in that piece of information. Their strategy on how to handle what had happened had gone as far as a lockdown. This was very understandable in the circumstances, but Jesus had been left out of the picture. Their strategy had been entirely based on fear. Then suddenly he comes and stands among them, in the middle of their fear, and says *'Peace be with you.'* (John 20:19, 21)

He knew these were the first words they needed to hear. Jesus hadn't abandoned the first disciples and he hasn't abandoned us either. He comes and stands among us.

No wonder the disciples needed to hear those words, *'Peace be with you'*. Perhaps this figure standing among them was a ghost? But he showed them his hands and side, and then they were convinced He really was there with them - raised from the dead; and they were totally overjoyed (John 20:20)! What a turnaround in feelings! Their emotions were all over the place. Luke says in his gospel that they were *'unable to believe for joy and amazement'* (Luke 24:41).

FACTUALLY BASED

The joy of those first locked-in disciples wasn't all froth and bubble, based on wishful thinking. Jesus had shown them his hands and feet, and they had touched him. Luke's gospel records that he even ate some fish in front of them in order to convince them (Luke 24:441-42). Ghosts don't eat fish. We may not have been there that day but there is a factual base to our belief that Jesus rose from the dead. The gospel accounts are there to reassure us that his resurrection really did happen. He was able to convince even doubting Thomas, when he appeared to them again a week later; this time with Thomas present. *'Jesus said to Thomas, "You have believed because you have seen me; blessed are those who have not seen me and yet have believed"* (John 20:29).

PROCESSING

When Jesus saw Thomas, a whole week had gone by since his first appearance to the other disciples. A week can be a long time in lock down. The disciples were still processing. He was there before their eyes and they could still hardly process it. We can almost hear them exclaiming, 'Unbelievable!'

In our lockdown we have been having our own experiences of processing what has been going on. There has been a lot to take in! Jesus is saying to us, *'Stop doubting and believe. I have risen from the dead, and I am with you now.'* He wants us to have confidence that he is not a myth. There are the facts of history – we can read about what they witnessed - the empty tomb and the folded grave cloths, and the multiple witnesses who saw him alive and risen. Paul has a long list of them, for example, in 1 Corinthians chapter fifteen, including five hundred who saw Jesus at the same time!
We also have our own growing experience of his presence through the Spirit in us. The lockdown has been a time to reflect on and process our own personal experiences with him.

WITH US RIGHT TO THE END

We shouldn't be surprised then, by Jesus walking with us, supporting us in what's going on right now. He said to those first disciples, *'Surely I am with you always to the very end of the age'* (Matthew 28:20). Last time I looked on the calendar, the age to which Jesus is referring hadn't come to an end; when it does, I am sure, he will wrap it all up and be the last one to leave. In the new language we are learning from zoom meetings, he is the one on the button who will end the meeting for all participants! He will be the last one left in the room! In all the upheaval of the circumstances in which we are now living, Jesus is there with us, saying 'Peace be with you. I am really here. I'm not a myth. I'm not some kind of make-believe comfort blanket'. It's very reassuring.

WORDS OF PEACE AND COMFORT

The peace that Jesus brings is like a strong force coming upon us and allaying all our fears. I felt this need for his peace early on in the lockdown, when I realised that one of our daughters who is a nurse, was interacting in her hospital with covid-19 patients but, at that time, was being inadequately protected. Bad images of my daughter catching the virus and dying gripped hold of me. I'd just watched a short animation film which graphically detailed the way covid-19 kills people so that hadn't helped me, and the media news was laying it on thick with fear. Resting back in the peace of Jesus and taking my fears to him in prayer, was the only way for me to keep calm. These words from one of Paul's letters really helped me, *'Do not be anxious about anything, but in everything by prayer and petition with thanksgiving make your requests known to God, and the peace of God which passes all understanding will keep your hearts and minds in Christ Jesus'* (Philippians 4:6-7).

PERSONALISE AND DECLARE GOD'S WORD

Two psalms were particularly an immediate blessing - Psalm ninety-one and Psalm one hundred and twenty-one. In the first few days of the pandemic it seemed as if everyone was bringing these two psalms out of their storehouse of good Bible passages. They are full of words of comfort and reassurance that God is looking after us and helping us, and are always worth a read at any time. So it was the words of these psalms that I personalised in prayer. I would read them out slowly and personalise them by changing the sentences into first person plural. So for example, *'Surely He will save you from the fowler's snare and from the deadly plague'* (Psalm 91:3) became 'Surely, *You* will save *us* from the fowler's snare and from the deadly plague'.

As I have read these psalms they have become lovely declarations of God's peace and protection over my family, and those for whom God has prompted me to pray.

He who the Son sets free is
free indeed!

John 8:36

CHAPTER TWO
SENT OUT

There are things ahead out there into which Jesus is sending us; new circumstances which we will have to get to grips with.

SENT OUT FROM LOCKDOWN

When Jesus appeared to the locked in disciples in the upper room, he didn't just reassure them once. He repeats, *'Peace be with you'* a second time as well. Something was coming up next which was also going to need them to rest in his peace (John 20:21). They should have guessed! They had been on the move with Jesus for three and a half years, and had understood a little of how he behaved. At one time he had warned a would-be follower what would be ahead for him, as a lifestyle, if he did choose to follow Jesus.

'Foxes have holes and the birds of the air have nests but the Son of man has nowhere to lay his head.' (Luke 9:58).

The disciples had lived an itinerant lifestyle never knowing where they might be going next. There had been nothing static about following Jesus. He was always on the move with purpose and direction. So what Jesus said next shouldn't have been a surprise!

Jesus says, *'As the Father has sent me, I am sending you'* (John 20:21). They are paralysed by fear and behind locked doors, but instead of leaving them there, Jesus is giving them their marching orders! He commissions them for mission. They will be going in his name and authority, to the whole world. Jesus unpacks the mission further - they would be witnesses to His resurrection, not only in the city of Jerusalem but *'in all Judea and Samaria, and to the ends of the earth'* (Acts 1:8).

A NEW DIRECTION AND PURPOSE

The disciples were given a plan that is geographically huge, and way out there in terms of their emotional state at the time. No wonder they needed those words, *'Peace be with you'*. Jesus was giving them a wider tangible reassurance of peace for what was ahead. Rather than hiding away, he was sending them out.

I believe he is doing the same with us. He is there to reassure us in our fears with his peace, but he is also launching us out into a wider place. He is coming to where we are currently positioned and addressing our immediate emotional state, but he has new direction and purpose for us which will require us to move. Even as Jesus spoke those sending words to the first disciples, he is speaking them to us too. *'As the Father has sent me, so I am sending you'.*

ALLOW HIM TO MOVE YOU

We need to be prepared to move. This may not necessarily be a physical movement. God may want us to stay put and join in with what he is doing in our local community. But, before we breathe a sigh of relief, this may not be the case. God may have other plans for us and we may find ourselves travelling all over the place. It really is up to him. If God wants to send us somewhere, it's always best to go along with His plan.

However, whether we stay local or find ourselves somewhere else, we will still have moved. God is taking us on a sending journey, which starts with a movement of the heart. This may not be apparent to others but, nevertheless, our hearts will have moved and lined themselves up with God's will. He wants to shift our hearts out of paralysis into a new place of freedom and availability.

NO EXCEPTIONS

God hasn't made any one of us an exception regarding this command to be sent out. When Jesus said to his first disciples, 'As the Father sent me, so I am sending you', he was referring to all of them. There were no exceptions. During the lockdown period, I believe Jesus has been using this period to reawaken his church to their role, their calling in the world. He has been re-commissioning us and helping us to regain a sense of who we really are. He has been reaffirming his commitment to us, right at the moment when we may have felt the least qualified.

The first disciples were locked down, shut up in fear. They were traumatised by what had gone on. They were terribly aware of how they'd behaved at the cross, and ashamed that they'd run away and denied Jesus. The good reports coming in of his resurrection hadn't lifted them out of unbelief and fear. Mark chapter sixteen catalogues their failure to believe, in spite of the witnesses.

'Jesus rebuked them for their lack of faith and stubborn refusal to believe those who had seen him after he had risen' (Mk 16:14).

But Jesus came and stood amongst them, commissioning them for their work ahead with him. He was prepared to be with them and he is prepared to be with us as well. Hebrews chapter two says that Jesus is not ashamed to call us his brothers (Heb 2:11).

WE ALL HAVE A PART TO PLAY

We mustn't let any sense of inadequacy keep us from doing our unique part. Our original plan for this season had been to spend time in Australia visiting one of our grown up sons and his family. How different that would have been from what has actually gone on! When we realised our trip was no longer possible, we were, understandably, very disappointed. There was a sense of loss. What we had been anticipating for so long had been removed in a moment. Like the disciples, the temptation to just hunker down at home and lick our wounds was quite strong. However, we began to sense that God was prompting us to help in different ways in the village community around us. As we began to do so, disappointment left us, and we happily got on with being part of God's plan for us. There was no point in looking back at what could have been.

There are some particular things that we have done over this time, which I am so pleased we have had the opportunity to do. It has been very satisfying to see, for example, local community organisations, including the churches, come together to form a mutual aid group in our local Northumberland village. Mary and I have also enjoyed getting to know some of the locals better, as we got involved in delivering weekly meals. They had been cooked by one of the ladies in the village, who herself had chosen to stay isolated at home. God's plan had been to send us out to help in the community, even in the middle of lockdown.

THE CIRCUMSTANCES HAVE CHANGED

Since the lockdown began, circumstances have changed. He is launching us out into new circumstances. Our communities are different. They are not the same as they were before the pandemic - they also have moved! There is a whole new geography out there which hasn't been mapped yet. Like the mariners of old, we will have to look upwards to the heavens to get our bearings on where we are, and how we are to navigate what lies ahead. However, in our communities, or wherever else we go, it will be with His sending authority behind us, and words of peace for what is ahead.

'I will lift up my eyes to the hills – where does my help come from? My help comes from the Lord, the Maker of heaven and earth' (Psalm 121:1)

'So we fix our eyes not on what is seen but on what is unseen. For what is seen is temporary but what is unseen is eternal' (2 Cor. 4:18).

'Fix your eyes upon Jesus' (Heb 12:2).

CHAPTER THREE
REASSEMBLED

Jesus is showing us new ways of doing things. The Holy Spirit has reassembled us to make us more effective in proclaiming the gospel of the forgiveness of sins.

WE NEED A HELPER

Behind locked doors, Jesus breathed on the first disciples and said, *'Receive the Holy Spirit'* (John 20:22). He knew the presence of the Holy Spirit would be needed. Without the Spirit they could do nothing. The Holy Spirit would make all the difference. How could they be sent without God being with them? Their situation, humanly speaking, was hopeless. Their leader had been crushed and they were a handful of largely uneducated Galileans facing the sophisticated wheelers and dealers of metropolitan Jerusalem politics. More bad news was ahead. They didn't know yet but Jesus would soon be ascending to Heaven, and his visible resurrection presence would no longer be with them.

A SPIRIT OF POWER

Jesus had already said to his disciples before His death that he would be sending the Holy Spirit who he describes as the Helper. Jesus had said to them *'It is for your good that I am going away - unless I go away, the Helper will not come to you'* (John 16:7). These were his final words before his ascension, according to Acts chapter one, *'but you will receive power when the Holy Spirit comes on you, and you will be my witnesses ....to the ends of the earth'* (Acts 1:8). They were to wait in Jerusalem until they had been *'clothed with power from on high'* (Luke 24:49). God's strength within them was the only way they were going to be able to fulfil the commission that Jesus had given them. There was no way they could be sent successfully without God's help. So after Jesus had ascended, they waited together in Jerusalem and when the day of Pentecost came a few days later, they were finally filled with the Holy Spirit, and immediately began to preach powerfully about Jesus with signs and miracles (Acts 2:4).

Similarly, as Jesus sends us out from this lockdown, we must be aware of the Spirit of God within us, and the power of God which is available through Him. Timothy is told by Paul, in 2 Tim.1:7, not to be fearful in the work he is doing, because he hasn't been given a spirit of fear but *'a spirit of power, of love and of a sound mind'*. We are being sent out from this lockdown in the same Spirit: of power, of love and of a sound mind.

A NEW CREATION IS BIRTHED

However, John chapter twenty is describing an earlier moment before the Spirit's coming in power at Pentecost. Jesus stood among the disciples and breathed on them, saying 'Receive the Holy Spirit'. This was something new and different to what they would experience later when they were baptised in the Spirit at Pentecost and received His power.

Within the locked room, a new creation was coming into being. Genesis describes the first man's creation in these terms, *'The Lord God formed the man from the dust of the earth and breathed into his nostrils the breath of life'* (Gen 2:7). In both the Hebrew and Greek languages used in the Bible, the word for Spirit and the word for breath are one and the same ('ruach' in Hebrew, 'pneuma' in Greek). So when the first man had been formed, one could as easily understand that the spirit of life had been breathed into his nostrils not just some oxygen! In a similar way, in the locked room a creative moment was taking place. Jesus was taking hold of the disciples and forming them into a new body, and then breathing the Holy Spirit on them.

They would never be the same again.

REASSEMBLED BONES

A vision of the prophet, Ezekiel illustrates the same idea. In Ezekiel chapter thirty-seven, Ezekiel has a vision of a valley of dry bones. The bones are very dry and scattered on the floor of a valley. In the vision, God tells Ezekiel that they represent the whole House of Israel (Ezek 37:11), and asks him whether these bones can live again. He replies, *'O Sovereign Lord, you alone know'*. Then God tells Ezekiel to prophesy to the bones so that they will live - that He will reassemble them, bones and tendons, flesh and skin, and put breath in them. In the vision, Ezekiel does this, and straight away there is a noise and a rattling sound and the bones come together, with their tendons, flesh and skin. Each bone is exactly where it should be. Finally as the breath enters their bodies the people come to life. The breath in the vision can again be understood to be the Spirit of God. (Ezek 37:14) God's Spirit had brought the people of Israel back to life.

NEW WAYS OF COMMUNICATING

During the covid-19 lockdown, we have experienced a sudden atomisation of our normal groupings within the global church. We have been forced through lockdown into our individual homes. Each home has become a single cellular unit of the whole, each of us isolated, scattered and unable to see one another face to face. We may have felt lost and torn apart from our normal friendship circles.

Suddenly, we have all gone online! However, meeting online as a church hasn't been the same as a physical church meeting. New creative ways of communicating have come into being, that were not being utilised beforehand. Conferences that would have taken months to organise have come together in a week. When we had better access physically, our online communications had been more marginal, but with no physical access possible at all, going online to communicate has suddenly become an absolute priority for everyone.

Over the last few months, Mary and I, for example, have been involved in hosting a range of meetings which I would never have considered creating before. We have brought together the most unlikely configurations of people for online times of sharing and prayer. One event we hosted, called 'Back to First Love', brought together elements of the church from all across the global time zones. The event was only forty-five minutes long yet gathered Christians in the same 'room' from places as far away from one another as Tahiti and Taiwan. In our isolated homes we were suddenly more together with the whole church than we would have ever previously bothered to be. Just for a moment, as we met together, we were representing the whole church across the globe, and giving voice to her desire to be flowing once again in her first love for God.

WITH NEW EYES AND EARS

Over the lockdown period, we sense that the church has been opened up to new ways of being. Elements of the church which normally would have been too busy in their local groups, have come together across the globe, and have found agreement with one another in prayer for future mission. God has been busy reconfiguring and reassembling the church during this lockdown time. He has destabilised and shaken us out of our routine patterns, and behind our locked doors, the individual bones have found themselves in a global womb, being brought together in novel and mission-effective ways. God has reassembled us, with brand new eyes and ears, to see and hear what had previously been invisible to us, was beyond our imagination, and our willingness to discover.

EMERGING TO BE MORE EFFECTIVE

Some of us prior to lockdown were in a bad way. The mission wasn't really going anywhere. We had been engaged mostly in a holding exercise, managing declining resources and decreasing congregations. On a personal level, some of us were burnt out and more than ready to forget the whole enterprise of mission. We were broken and scattered, shattered and destroyed. Our bones were all over the floor of the valley.

Amazingly, God has rearranged things and got our attention. He has come for us, and because He loves us, and the whole world, in all its rebellion, He has wooed us back into His master plan. We might be looking atomised and individuated, but actually we are now right where God wants us to be. He is doing the positioning and I sense that on the other side of lockdown, we are going to emerge with His breath in our reassembled lungs, looking leaner and fitter!

I FORGIVE YOUR SINS

'If you forgive anyone their sins, they are forgiven. If you do not forgive them, they are not forgiven' (John 20:23).
These are the words that Jesus spoke to the first disciples in the locked room. Jesus' assertion that he had the authority to absolutely forgive a person's sins was a radical statement that had set off into a tizz the religious leaders of his day. During his public ministry, he had spoken words of forgiveness over a paralytic, for example, when he healed him (Matthew 9:1-8). The teachers of the Law were incensed - *'This fellow is blaspheming'* was their reaction. In Israel, people at that time were supposed to go to the Temple priesthood and the sacrificial system to have their sins covered, and here was Jesus declaring to people with an authority straight from heaven that their sins were forgiven.

A MINISTRY OF RECONCILIATION

In the locked room after the resurrection, Jesus was now investing authority in His followers to also forgive sins. This wasn't about forgiveness on a human level only – a reconciliation, for example, between people who have fallen out with one another. It is an absolute forgiveness of sins with all the authority of God. Jesus was saying that, in his authority and name, those who followed him were now being sent out into the world to proclaim an offer of reconciliation with God.

'...He gave us the ministry of reconciliation that God was reconciling the world to Himself in Christ, not counting men's sins against them...' (2 Corinthians 5:18-19). Along with the apostle John, he wants us to have the confidence to tell people -
'If we confess our sins, He is faithful and just, and will forgive us our sins and purify us from all unrighteousness.' (I John 1:9).

In the locked room the sacrifice was standing in front of them, Jesus Christ. The sacrifice had been made. He had taken away the sins of the world. The disciples had assembled in fear behind a locked door thinking it best to keep their heads down, but Jesus had broken through all that. He had breathed on them, saying, *'Receive the Holy Spirit'*, and was sending them all out with the message of forgiveness. This is the message with which we are also being sent out, from our own lockdowns - that there is forgiveness of sins through Jesus. *'He is the atoning sacrifice for our sins, and not only ours, but also for the sins of the whole world'* (1 John 2:2).

NEW RELATIONSHIPS

New patterns of relationship have emerged during the lockdown period. It is important therefore, that as we move forward, we don't rush back into our church buildings, but look at ways in which mission might be better done, through the new online relationships that we have made. We may have also rediscovered our immediate physical neighbours in our streets, and noticed an increased level of neighbourly good will in our communities. Your presence might be a blessing to them - through you, they may get to hear about the God who loves them. This may be a challenge, if we have been offended by our neighbours, or had disputes with them. This period is an opportunity to put that behind you, and decide to exercise forgiveness. If we examine our hearts, we may discover where we have got it wrong ourselves. We can hardly proclaim God's message of forgiveness if we are refusing to forgive!

Life Breath

Life Breath

You are my life and my breath

Jesus, You are my ventilator

I trust in You alone.

Help me every day,

With every breath, I worship You-

The Living Breath,

Your Holy Spirit,

Your Presence LIVING in me!

Wonderful Breath of God

Breathe in me, breathe through me-

LIFE, LIFE, LIFE!

Into the atmosphere,

Changing the landscape,

Saving lives,

Delivering the captives!

Come, come Living Breath;

Ruach-Spirit Wind

Blow upon this Nation.

We welcome You!

Written early on in the Lockdown and partly inspired while listening to 'This is the air I breathe' by Michael W Smith.

Mary Bain March 2020

PART TWO

LOCKDOWN LESSONS

CHAPTER FOUR
LESSONS TO LEARN

We have had something to learn in our lockdown experience. We may be slow but God is patient and will complete the work He has begun in us.

FORTY YEARS IN THE WILDERNESS

The People of Israel were about to take possession of the land the Lord had given them. They had been in the wilderness, and now it was time to launch out into what the Lord had for them. We can read about this moment in the early chapters of Deuteronomy, and onwards into the rest of that book. In Deuteronomy, Moses recaps what has gone on in the wilderness over forty years, and gets the people of God ready for their own launch out from their lockdown there. It's a very long speech – a lot can go on over forty years in someone's life; even more so in the life of a nation!

NEW THINGS TO LEARN

Recalling all that has gone on over forty years of our life may be beyond us, but it may be helpful to reflect over the last few months, and consider what lessons we may have been learning. This is always a good discipline. This year, at the start of a Lent lunch in our nearby town, a church leader, giving the thought for the day, suggested that rather than giving up something for Lent we learnt something instead. Little did we realise the kind of things we would be learning! We have learnt, for example, a whole new raft of online skills, with media platforms like zoom. In tidying up our children's old Lego kits to give to our grandchildren, I have learnt that every single type of missing Lego brick has an order code! We have got busy on some domestic projects, and have lost some weight through daily exercises. I don't think we have ever walked so much every day before! Most of all, the steadier routine that has been put in place, has simplified our lifestyles, and freed up time, that we did not have previously. Mary and I have had to really examine our priorities in how we use that time, and it has exposed just how little, or how much, we really want to live our lives closely with the God we love. The really important lessons are, after all, how we handle our hearts. I wonder if this has been the same for you too?

THE WHOLE WORLD IS LEARNING SOMETHING!

I admire Moses' perseverance with the people of Israel. He knew there were some important lessons of the heart which they needed to learn, and take with them out of their time in the wilderness. I don't think I would have wanted his job. A lockdown for just a few weeks may seem trivial in comparison, time wise, to forty years in the wilderness, but what has gone on in 2020 has been global in scope and not at all trivial - an experience shared not by just one nation, but by the whole world, and a learning time for everybody. Although dealing with a different time frame of experiences, what we have been experiencing has been one of epic Biblical proportions. So these early chapters of Deuteronomy do seem to be an appropriate part of God's word for us to consider at this time, and to learn from.

SHAKEN OUT

The world has been in a wilderness experience, shaken out from its normal routines. This was the experience of the people of God in the wilderness. They had come out from what had been their normal lives - an experience of slavery and oppression in Egypt. They had groaned about it, but they didn't really expect anything to change. Deuteronomy describes a people who had gone through a destabilising experience. They had lost their old certainties, and after being in the wilderness, were about to step out across the river Jordan to find a new normal. We can learn from them as we prepare for what lies ahead beyond our own wilderness experiences. We too will be stepping out into something new.

SLOW LEARNERS

The people of God were learning in the wilderness for forty years which suggests that they were probably slow learners! We may also be slow learners, or maybe not so slow, but the first step in our launching out after lockdown is to realise that there really are some actual lessons for us to learn and take with us. Has God been teaching us something? We could be in the wilderness a long time, if

Shaken Out ...

we are so dim-witted that we don't realise that this is a learning period. I am amazed at God's patience with us. Like Moses, He knows the material with which He is working, and yet He still continues with us. His work goes beyond just the long speeches we find Moses making in Deuteronomy. It is much more hands-on. It should be no surprise to us to see the prophet Jeremiah describing God in terms of a potter working with his lumps of clay on a potter's wheel (Jeremiah 18:6).

THE PATIENT WORK OF GOD

The schools may have been closed and our children may be struggling to adjust to a different environment. In lockdown they may not have realised that home could be just as much a learning environment as a classroom at school. In the same way, it may have all seemed intolerable and impossible for us to learn new things at home in lockdown. But in the midst of all the noise and cafuffle, our children have been learning something, and so have we! Like parents home-schooling their own children, God has been patiently at work with us, opening us up to some new thoughts and bringing us into a new place. The environment may not have looked particularly conducive, the material He is working with may not have seemed up to much, but in His skilful hands, for all eyes to see, new pots <u>are</u> emerging. We are being shaped by the Potter more than we may realise, during and through this very different time.

CHAPTER FIVE
GOD IS BEHIND THE LOCKDOWN

God is behind the lockdown. We need to trust in what He is doing with us and the nations and not get frightened or angry.

For the people of God in Deuteronomy, their lockdown in the wilderness had been imposed on them by God Himself. They were there for forty years wandering in the desert because God would not allow them to move forward into the land which He had promised them, until a whole new generation had grown up. Finally, when God gave the signal, they were released out of the wilderness to make their way to the river Jordan, and beyond to the Promised land. God's hand in what they went through was front and back stage. He was continually working with them, constant throughout the forty years, and they all knew and understood that.

The lockdown which we have experienced was imposed on us by the responses of national governments to a worldwide pandemic. Those in charge knew that something must be done and made their individual responses to the crisis. God doesn't seem to have featured in any way in their decision-making. We might conclude then, that we are in very different times, and that there is nothing relevant for us to look at in the Bible, to help us in what we are experiencing now. What has this lockdown got to do with God?

However, God has not gone away in the intervening centuries since Moses, and the nation of Israel with him, stood on the edge of something new, by the river Jordan. Nothing has changed!
God has been involved in His creation in every century since that time, and He is still at work now. Ultimately, we have to say that God has been behind the lockdown.

GOD IS WITH US

Whatever we are currently experiencing cannot be analysed only from a human perspective, once we comprehend that God is with us. If we look with different eyes, we can sense that God's hand is directing the affairs of the nations on the earth now, and that His purposes are unfolding in all that has been going on, even up to today. On a personal level, God is with us in the detail as well. If Jesus is right that our Heavenly Father feeds the sparrows and knows the number of hairs on our heads (Luke 12:6-7), then we can be sure that He understands and is involved in the detail of our own personal lockdown. His guiding hand has been at work every day, in every circumstance and every experience we have gone through.

The Psalms proclaim that *'The earth is the Lord's and everything in it, the world and all who live in it'* (Psalm 24:1).
God is watching over the whole world and nothing is being overlooked by Him. We can believe that God has been leading us in and through this lockdown, and that whatever launching out of lockdown may look like, ultimately, He will be directing all the details of that as well.

TRUST IN THE LORD

When we know that God is behind this lockdown, we can then begin to believe the truth expressed by Joseph, in the book of Genesis, that whatever had been meant for evil, God will turn round for good (Gen 50:20). We need to trust that He knows what He is doing, and that we don't need to be anxious or fearful. I love these words from Proverbs chapter three, *'Trust in the Lord with all your heart and lean not on your own understanding. In all your ways acknowledge Him and He will direct your path. Do not be wise in your own eyes, Fear the Lord and depart from evil'* (Proverbs 3:5-7). The challenge for us is to put our trust in the One who made us, despite the fact that everything around us has suddenly and completely changed.

HE UNDERSTANDS US

God doesn't want us to be full of fear. Isaiah chapter forty-one records these lovely words, spoken out especially for us. *'Fear not, for I am with you. Be not dismayed, for I am your God. I will strengthen you, I will help you, I will uphold you with my victorious right arm'* (Isa 41:10). God understands our make-up. He knows our weaknesses and our limits, and promises to help and strengthen us.

TRAINING TO GO IN A NEW DIRECTION

Our hearts have been undergoing a change of direction during the lockdown. When I was a teenager, during the school holidays, I would work in the glasshouses near our family home. They were growing cucumbers and tomatoes there. One of the jobs we used to do, early in the growing season, was to lift the cucumber plants off the ground and turn them very gently around strings, which we had tied vertically on to the glasshouse frame. Left to their own devices the cucumbers would have spread out in a terrible tangle, horizontally in the dirt.

Like the cucumbers, God has been lifting us up in the direction He wants for our lives, during this lockdown. He has been gently handling us, so we get used to a different orientation. What an amazing difference it makes to go God's way! Previously we may have been making do, handling our spiritual life in any old fashion, drawing on both helpful and unhelpful places to sustain us. If we have been grubbing around in the dirt, gaining comfort from things that we really know are bad habits and routines, now is the time to drop them, and not to go back!

NO LOOKING BACK

So beyond the lockdown, there must be no grumbling and no looking back at something that now looks sweet from a distance, and that you could imagine still had a pleasurable side. This is what the people of God in the wilderness began to do, as they remembered, with rose-tinted spectacles, how life had been in Egypt, before God had brought them out. In reality whatever fleeting pleasures there had been in Egypt, their lives had been lived under oppression, slavery and destruction. There was nothing on offer in Egypt that would in reality have helped them get through the wilderness.

GOD IS INTERESTED IN NATIONS

God has not finished with the United Kingdom. I was reading some very dismissive words about our spiritual state, which could be true of any nation in the western world. Based on our current behaviour as a nation, the commentator said, we were no longer a Christian society, not even a post-Christian one, but pre-Christian. In his analysis, there was nothing left in our society on which the gospel message was able to land. This is a bleak assessment and could leave us feeling very hopeless about where our society is heading - how it might look in another ten or twenty years time. However, God has a long memory, and He has a strong love towards any nation which has made covenants with Him. The United Kingdom has a history of doing this. Our monarch has made promises that she will rule with God's help. She is still the temporal Head of the state church. Our national flag bears witness to this in all its inter-crossed crosses. The whole nation is prayed for regularly by the state church, parish by parish. There is still a canopy of blessing over us, more than we may realise.

God says these words to the prophet, Jeremiah, *'I am watching to see that my word is fulfilled'* (Jeremiah 1:12).
He has a long memory and isn't derailed in His plans by any passing silliness we may be engaged in as nation. He knows very well how far away certain elements of our nation are from Him. However, because of His love and faithfulness towards the United Kingdom, He wants to bring us into fruitfulness, and our particular place in His ordering of the affairs of the nations. He has plans for our nation as He does for every nation of the world. On a personal level also, He has charged us to look after our own part of the earth assigned to us, and to be fruitful. We do this using the unique skills and opportunities He has given to us.

HE TRANSFORMS EVIL INTO BLESSING

If we haven't thought about any of this recently or ever, then this period of lockdown has been a time to reset our thinking. God wants us to understand He has been in the lockdown and His plans and purposes are being worked out across the whole earth. We mustn't get our thinking befuddled by the noise of the enemy with his schemes to steal, kill and destroy (John 10:10). Whatever he meant for evil, whether directly or through human agency or natural causes, God is turning round for our greater good and blessing (Genesis 50:20). God has the final word on the pandemic we have experienced, and all that we have ever undergone. As someone has said, regarding the Bible – 'I have looked at the back of the book, and the good news is, we win!' This is the reassurance everyone can have who puts their trust in God.

CHAPTER SIX
JESUS IN THE WILDERNESS

We can learn from Jesus' own experience in the wilderness just before his launch into public ministry. This is a key time to settle what is really important in our lives, and to birth new ideas and projects.

LED BY THE SPIRIT

The Spirit of God led Jesus out into the wilderness immediately after his baptism by John, right at the beginning of his public ministry. The Holy Spirit obviously considered it necessary for Jesus to go through this experience. He was taking Jesus away from all his usual surroundings and interactions and giving him an extended period of isolation. He was forty days alone and without food. Except he wasn't alone. Mark's gospel tells us that the Spirit sent Jesus into the desert, and that he was there in the desert for forty days being tempted by Satan, that he was there with the wild animals, and that angels attended him (Mark 1:12-13). So in the desert, Jesus encounters Satan as well as wild animals and angels. Quite a crowd! Human company was taken away from him. He was stripped of all the noise of that, but different challenges were revealed, of a different order. Satan was there to tempt him. There were the wild animals, and finally, after that, there were the angels to help him. Matthew chapter four says that after the temptations, *'the devil left him and angels came and attended him'* (Matt 4:11).

In the wilderness, Jesus was kept safe from the dangers of the wild animals, and perhaps there is even a suggestion, in the passage from Mark's gospel, that he was living peacefully with them, enjoying the creation of God around him. The angels were there to help and strengthen him. The encounter with Satan had a victorious conclusion, but clearly had left Jesus drained and in need of their help.

DWELLING ON DEUTERONOMY

Interestingly, Deuteronomy is the part of scripture that Jesus was thinking about, during the forty days he spent in the wilderness.

Deuteronomy chapters six and eight specifically, are the only bits of the Bible from which he openly quotes, in the written accounts about his time in the wilderness (Matthew 4:1-11). In fact they form the basis of his replies to the temptations presented by Satan. Jesus picks out key foundational truths from Deuteronomy and counters every move of the enemy.

For every temptation from Satan, Jesus has a reply.
The devil says to him, 'Tell these stones to become bread.'
Jesus says, *'It is written, Man does not live on bread alone but on every word that comes from the mouth of God'* (Deut 8:3).
The devil says, 'Throw yourself down from the highest point of the Temple – you will be safe.'
Jesus says, *'It is also written, Do not put the Lord your God to the test'* (Deut 6:16).
The devil says, 'Bow down and worship me and I will give you the kingdoms of the world and their splendour.'
Jesus says, *'It is written, Worship the Lord your God and serve Him only'* (Deut 6:13)
Looking at his replies it is clear that Jesus had settled in his heart what was really important.

How appropriate that Jesus, in his own time of lockdown in the wilderness, should consider the experiences of the people of God in the wilderness, all those years before. This was a launching place moment for Jesus, just as it had been for them. They were about to move out across the Jordan into the land God had promised to them. Here was Jesus, in the same locality as his forefathers all those years before. He had been led into the wilderness by the Holy Spirit immediately after his baptism by John in the river Jordan, and now he was about to commence his public ministry in Judea and Galilee. From now on, he would be in the public gaze and would have to manage all that would accompany that.

Out of his own experiences in the wilderness, Jesus was about to launch into the purposes of God across the other side of the river Jordan. No wonder he was thinking about the experience of the people of God in Deuteronomy.

FOCUS IS KEY

There is always a need to listen and tune in to God's plans and purposes for our lives, and not get distracted. No wonder the devil tempted Jesus in the wilderness. He hates new life and fruitfulness, and this was an opportune time for him to abort and destroy the good work that lay ahead for Jesus, before it had even got started. Some of us have been easily distracted and lost our sense of direction. Being in lockdown has given us a place to examine ourselves in a more simplified environment than our normal one. We have had an opportunity to settle within ourselves what is important to us. The old distractions have been taken away.

KEEP THE MAIN THING THE MAIN THING!

So what is important to us? When Jesus was asked this question, Mark's gospel records that he replied, quoting these words from Deuteronomy 6:5, *'Love the Lord your God with all your heart and with all your soul, and with all your mind, and with all your strength'* (Mark 12:30). This is a very comprehensive response, which challenges us on every level of our being. Nothing is intended to be left out of our launch from lockdown. God is dealing with us comprehensively. Our hearts, souls, minds and strength are all to be involved. Ahead of us, if we will allow it, is a love engagement with God like we've never thought was possible before. Jesus came out from those forty days in the wilderness, close to his Heavenly Father and strengthened by the experience. This is also God's intention for us - that we will launch out from lockdown with our hearts close to Him and in a stronger place.

BACK TO BASICS

In the wilderness, Jesus experienced a time where much of his normal life had been stripped away and he was totally dependent on God, his Father. To varying degrees, this may have been our experience at this time as well.

We have really enjoyed going back to the basics. Normally our church work involves us travelling around a lot, and meeting up with people in coffee shops, or being indoors making telephone calls or writing e-mails. Suddenly all the travelling has stopped and we have been entirely home-based. Fortunately, we are living in a lovely part of the country, and there are plenty of nice walks to enjoy. Also, although our garden isn't enormous, we have made it into a prayer garden called 'Albafarne', and it is affiliated to the Quiet Garden Trust. Ordinarily, people can come to visit the garden and spend time out from the busyness of life; they can slow down, breathe deeply and enjoy resting in God's presence. Of course during the lockdown the garden has been closed. However, during this time, we have begun to realise that we hadn't been so good ourselves at breathing deeply, resting in God's presence and spending time just listening to the birds. We are trying to set that straight, and also take some time out, to appreciate the beauty of God's creation all around us. It is not impossible, even in the most urban environments, to do this. God has His breathing spaces for us in unexpected places. He wants us to explore with open eyes and enjoy time out.

VALUE EACH DAY

We are great Jane Austen fans, and have been reading her novel, Emma, and watching the TV adaptations as well. Emma lives in the confined world of Highbury, with her father, in a posh house called Hartfield. In a way, she is in her own contented lockdown. For her it is a big deal to plan a day out with a picnic. She has never been to the sea. She never moves out of Highbury throughout the novel. Austen captures the language of the people in Emma's world extremely well. One very talkative lady, Miss Bates, for example, spends pages talking about the most ordinary of foods - baked apples! Although nothing much appears to be happening – there is no high drama –yet we are taken on a journey which feels very full and satisfying. The whole book is a celebration of the ordinary and the every day, and in the end these things turn out to matter much more than the affairs of kings and queens! This has been a lesson we have learned at this time. God wants us to value the details of ordinary life, and celebrate them. We don't want to lose this perspective.

WITH THE WILD ANIMALS

There are also challenges and scares in the wilderness. Fear can run rampant as we listen to the media, and then we look round our home, and everything looks very normal. As one of our daughters said,

'We've joined up to fight against the corona virus and now what? What are we supposed to do?' It's been very hard to fight against an invisible enemy, in a battlefield that looks so ordinary. Out there the corona virus may be lurking somewhere in the wilderness, with all the other wild animals, and our trips to the shops for essentials could lead us into danger.

VALUE LIFE

We have had our own dangers with bigger 'wild' animals over the lockdown. One day we got more than we bargained for on a local walk in the countryside, when we met a herd of bullocks, hurtling down a slope towards us. We were on the right of way, coming up from a stream in the valley quite a distance from them, and had no intention of going anywhere near them, but they had seen us coming, and ran as a herd towards us. Fortunately, they lost their nerve at the last moment and veered away. We breathed a sigh of relief, but it felt like a close shave! The danger felt very real and very visible. An ordinary walk had turned into a nightmare. We climbed over the stile and escaped. The field behind us looked normal again, but we had actually had an extraordinary encounter with death there! The experience left us very thankful and appreciative that we were alive. There is nothing like a close call to make you value your life. As we come out of lockdown let us also be appreciative and thankful for our lives.

EXPECTANCY

In the wilderness, Jesus was hidden away from normal life. There were things he needed to gestate and birth spiritually, that needed the quiet and isolation in order to take place. The confinement ahead of the birth of a baby is a strange time. There is an expectation and an awareness of change. New life is being developed within, and we become aware that we will never be the same again after the baby is born. A profound change that has begun invisibly, will finally result in a birth that all will see. We don't understand how the baby will look or its character, and we may deliberately keep the gender a secret even to ourselves. However, the fact of an on-going development is undeniably and increasingly visible, even if we don't know yet all the answers, and the changes which are going to occur after the baby is born.

BIRTHING OF CREATIVITY

I believe there are babies that are being gestated and birthed out of this 2020 lockdown who will go on to be great blessings. These are not just human babies, although people are predicting a spike in births as a result of the lockdown! Creative ideas are being formed, business ideas are popping up into people's minds. Prototypes are being experimented with. A deep understanding of who we are, and what God wants of us, has been settling upon us. We believe, this is part of what God intended, and the flow of where the lockdown is taking us.

GOD IS HOVERING OVER US

There has been a hovering of the Spirit of God over the waters of the earth, even like that first day of creation described in Genesis chapter one. God has been declaring new things into being. He is saying, 'Let there be', and new frameworks are being formed and filled with amazing and wonderful things. Who could have imagined the wonders of creation ahead of its birthing? The frameworks God brought into being of sky and sea and land, and the beings that God then chose to fill them with. Today, He has words to speak over each one of us beyond our imagination. There are new frameworks that He wants us to operate in and fill with His amazing love and creativity. We mustn't be limited by our imaginations. The apostle, Paul writes in Ephesians chapter three, *'Now to Him who is able to do immeasurably more than all we ask or imagine, according to His power that is at work within us...'* (Eph 3:20). God's work in our lives is just amazing.

I AM A NEW CREATION

In 2 Corinthians chapter five, speaking about the new birth we experience, when we become followers of Jesus, Paul writes, *'Therefore if anyone is in Christ he is a new creation, behold the old has passed away, the new has come'* (2 Cor. 5:17). The devil just wanted to shut us down, and shut us up. His plan was to let the old pass away and to roll a stone over the entrance of our tombs. He wanted our love to grow cold, and for us to be hardened up inside of ourselves. But he didn't bargain on the love of God, which has pursued us, and the power contained within that love. When all seemed finished, and we were dead and buried, the Spirit of God hovered over us in the grief and mess of it all, and spoke life, and a new creation.

ANGELS IN ATTENDANCE

There have been people being rescued from spiritual death, every day during this lockdown. They have cried out in desperation. They have ached for love. The experience of being shut down and caged in, has given them a focussed understanding of their need for the new life which only Jesus can bring. A new ache to drink in God's love has seized hold of them.

The number of people searching for 'Prayer' on Google has skyrocketed. Large numbers of Bibles have also been sold and hopefully, people are reading them. We had a random request ourselves, the other day, for a Bible from someone we have known for a few years. Suddenly, in the lockdown, he has wanted to read the Bible. In the privacy of shutdown, people have also dared to listen in to online church services, and have actually heard for the first time that Jesus is the answer to all the questions they have had about their lives, but never dared to ask before.

The prophet, Isaiah, wrote these words, *'Come, all you who are thirsty, come to the waters; and you who have no money, come, buy and eat! Come, buy wine and milk without money and without cost'* (Isaiah 55:1).

Just as God sent angels to help Jesus in the wilderness, and uses them even today, He can also send us as part of his plan, to reach those who are weary and crying out for help. We heard of a lovely example of a man in an Intensive Care Unit who was recovering from the virus. Strangely, he was imagining how nice it would be to have a packet of Prawn cocktail crisps and a can of coke. No visitors were allowed, so this seemed impossible, and he didn't mention it to anyone. The cleaner, who he knew was a Christian, amazingly popped by, a little while later, with something in a carrier bag, as a gift for him. When he looked inside the bag, there was a can of coke and a packet of Prawn cocktail crisps! Let's be available to listen to God's promptings and be kind in the small details of people's lives.

CHAPTER SEVEN
REPENTANCE

The restoration of our relationship with God starts with repentance. This is why Jesus died on the cross for our sins and rose from the dead. God holds out the invitation for us to come back home, completely forgiven of all our sins.

In this strange time, when we are keeping our distance from everyone else, Jesus is knocking on our door and wants us to invite him in.

READY TO MEET GOD

Just before the time in the desert, Jesus had come down to the river Jordan, where John was baptising people with a baptism of repentance. People were coming to John the Baptist to be baptised from all over the region. The bottom line was that John wanted people to be ready for an encounter with God, and repentance was a precursor to that. This was not just a moment for people to say sorry for a few specific things that they had messed up on. This was a moment for them to change their entire life's direction; a moment to totally change their thinking about God, and turn back to Him; to positively move towards Him, rather than away from Him. This is what repentance really means. They came to John wanting to be ready to meet God, and getting wet in the water of the river Jordan was an outward way of marking that inward intention of the heart.

We may not have recognised, as we entered into lockdown, that this might be a serious moment to consider our own repentance. However, this has been God's intention. He has wanted to bring each of us to a place where we are prepared to turn towards Him, and repent. In a moment we can change our entire life's direction. In a moment, we can completely change our thinking about God, and positively move towards Him.

ROADWORKS AHEAD!

John described himself as the one who had come to prepare the way for the Lord. He drew on prophetic words from Isaiah, chapter forty to describe his work.

'A voice of one calling in the desert, prepare the way for the Lord; make straight in the wilderness a highway for our God. Every valley shall be raised up, every mountain and hill made low; the rough ground shall become level, the rugged places a plain. And the glory of the Lord will be revealed, and all mankind together will see it...' (Isaiah 40:3-5)

These are road building words. The land being described in this passage is all over the place! There are dips and ravines, hilly bits and difficult terrains. In fact, this is quite a wilderness for any road to cross! We are not great road engineers when it comes to how our hearts work. However, God has been on our case. He knows all about our hearts, and has come to help us. Let's allow Him to do that heart preparation work in us, so that there is a clear highway for us to walk ahead in our lives, together with Him.

IF ANYONE HEARS MY VOICE

In Revelation 3:20, Jesus is described as standing at the door of our lives knocking, and awaiting our response. For those who positively respond and open the door, there is a promise from God that He will come into our lives. Revelation 3:20 says that He promises *'to come in and eat with us, and be with us'*. He doesn't expect us to get the house all tidy before we open the door. In fact He is a dab hand with a hoover, and can help us to put the kettle on, and sit down with a biscuit or two! The action of opening the door requires the same decision of the heart that led people to go down to the river Jordan, to be baptised by John. Beyond the door is a new beginning and a launching out into a new life as a believer in Jesus Christ. During the lockdown period, God has been calling many of us to repent and open up our lives to Him.

JESUS WANTS TO COME INTO OUR HEARTS AND HOMES

One of the lockdown restrictions has been that no one who isn't family should enter our homes. We haven't opened the door and let anyone in at all. People have talked to us from a distance, or via the internet or telephone, but no-one has come in to sit down and have a cup of tea with us. We may have thought ourselves very much alone. But actually, God has been with us. As we read earlier, God is in the house, and His presence makes all the difference! If we have, to date, neglected to invite Him into our heart and our home, then this is our moment to do so.

We can pray this simple prayer:-

Dear Jesus, I turn to you, I am sorry for having kept you outside of my life.
Thank you for dying on the cross for me. Thank you for coming after me, and knocking on the door of my heart.
I am opening the door now, and say, 'Welcome into my life'. May your presence change me forever. May I never be the same again.
Today, I choose to stick with you, and follow you always. Amen.'

CHAPTER EIGHT
GOD IS WOOING US

God wants our relationship with him restored. We have been distracted by deceptions but finally we have the desire to put our lives right with God.

MY HOPE IS IN YOU

God has been leading us to a point where we will say, 'My hope is in you, and in no other' (incidentally the title words of one my favourite songs by Thomas Tallis – 'Spem in alium'). We have a terrible ability to put our hopes in all sorts of things other than God. One wonders what it will take for the souls of men, women, and children to come to the point of putting their hope only in God! The book of Hosea tells of God's love for His people, in terms of a husband wanting to restore the relationship with his wayward wife.

THE PRODIGAL WIFE

We are probably all familiar with the story of the Prodigal Son coming back to his father (see Luke chapter 15). Ultimately the son's hunger moves him. *'My father's servants are better looked after than this ...with food to spare'* (Luke 15:17). Less well known is the story of the Prodigal wife, we read about in Hosea chapter two. She thinks her provision, what she desperately needs to satisfy her sense of wellbeing, lies in having relationships with other men, apart from her husband. She thinks they will provide her with her food and water, her wool and linen, her oil and her drink (Hosea 2:5).But she finds herself thwarted in her pursuit, and ends up chasing after her lovers but never catching them. She looks for them, but never finds them (Hosea 2:7). In spite her misguided best efforts, her sexual escapades come to nothing. Like the Prodigal son, it is at this point that she makes a decision to return home, and says, *'I will go back to my husband as at first, for then I was better off than now'* (Hosea 2:7).

In realising that this story is really all about God and His people, the truth can then be seen; that everything she's ever had were all His blessings to her in the first place! He had been the source of her provision all along. The grain, the new wine and the oil, the silver, the gold, the wool and the linen were all given to her out of the goodness of God's heart. Her waywardness had got her into deep trouble. So God leads her into the wilderness, to fall in love with him all over again.

'Therefore I am now going to woo her: I will lead her into the wilderness and speak tenderly to her. The vines and fig trees which were taken away and ruined, I will now give back to her, and the valley of Achor (which translated means trouble), I will make a door of hope.' (Hosea 2:14-15).

BACK TO FIRST LOVE

We may, like the Prodigal wife, have been in the wilderness and isolation of lockdown, and then been surprised to discover that God has been seeking us there. This may apply to you! Do you sense that God has been on your case, pulling you back to your senses? In the busyness and distractions of life, we may have neglected thinking about Him. Maybe we have never thought He was really there for us. In this extraordinary time He has been gracious enough to give us an opportunity, to discover afresh how much He really loves us.

The absence of our old routines of daily life prior to lockdown, has created in us a cry and an ache for something more. Is that what has been happening to you, and to the people around you? Personally, Mary and I have felt God's call to go deeper with Him, and have also prayed for many to come to God during this period. This is the season for all of us to hear God's heart of love.

THE SEASON OF SINGING

'There {in the wilderness] she will sing as in the days of her youth, as in the day she came up out of Egypt' (Hosea 2:15)
This is what happens when we come back to God – there is a song that bubbles up inside of us – it's a light, happy song of thankfulness to God. It's just such a lovely feeling of amazement that God has been with us all the time, and has brought about this wonderful change in our circumstances. Jesus says in John's gospel chapter ten, that he has come to bring abundant life (John 10:10).
This has been my experience through all the ups and downs of life, in my best moments, and my bleakest - God's abundance has been right there with me. I made the decision to follow Jesus when I was twenty years old, and have never regretted it. It has been the best decision I have ever made.

Some of us have believed in God for a while, but possibly haven't sung any songs recently. This season is a good time to begin. Don't be put off by what others might think in the house. Sing in the shower, in the kitchen, or when you're doing the ironing. We have something to be thankful for, even in a difficult time like this.

RESETTING OUR HEARTS

One night during the lockdown, I was given a word from God while I was asleep. It wasn't like I was hearing a booming voice from Heaven, but I just heard the words, Psalm eighty-five! This was so frustrating because I didn't know what that Psalm was about, and I kept thinking, 'I'm asleep, How will I remember this when I wake up?' But I did remember, and woke up eager to read it, knowing that there would be something to learn from it. The Psalm was very encouraging and just what I needed to hear at the time.

Psalm eighty-five is all about stepping out with God in a new day. The sun has come up, and this psalm is such a wonderful song from God, for us to sing back to Him. It is all about restoration. If we have messed things up, we can come back to God and ask Him to restore us- to reset our hearts. We may have been finding life difficult to handle, and looking to old habit patterns and ways of living to handle the tedium of it. One moment we can be sensing the closeness and wonder of the Lord's presence, and then exchange all that for some not very elevating rubbish on television, or other media. The lockdown has tested our hearts, and made us very aware of the clever deceptions of the enemy to sidetrack us. But then along comes the Spirit of God to rescue and restore, so that the enemy doesn't triumph over us. Just one touch from God changes everything.

'Restore us again, O God our Saviour' (Ps 85:4).
In Psalm 85:8-9, God promises peace to His people *'but let them not return to folly. Surely His salvation is near those who fear Him, that His glory may dwell in our land'* (Ps 85:12).

DON'T GET SIDETRACKED

The people of Israel were sidetracked by the enemy, just before they were set to launch out from their forty years of being in the wilderness. In the last part of their journey they had been unstoppable. Nothing was going to prevent them reaching the land God had promised to them.

Instead of attempting to attack them, a local king called Balak recognised that if the people of Israel were to be stopped, it would have to be away from the battlefield. A full-on assault by others had proved impossible. You can read this story in Numbers chapters twenty-two to twenty-five. Balak called in an occultist, Balaam, and asked him to curse the Israelites. The plan didn't get anywhere, because God intervened, and Balaam was unable to speak out anything but a blessing over them, but not for want of trying! He had his eye on the pay cheque from Balak, and advised another approach (Numbers 31:16). Send in the local women and seduce the Israelite men into their local fertility worship. This involved eating sacrifices to their fertility god, and then sealing the event with sex. The men fell for it, and a plague broke out which was only stopped by one of the Israelites, Phineas making a stand against it.

TWO TYPES OF SOUL FOOD

It is interesting that El Shaddai, (one of the Bible names for God) features heavily in the story of Balaam. This is the name for God which is especially associated with provision and spiritual nourishment. It's actually a very feminine name for God. The 'shad' in El Shaddai is the Hebrew word for a breast. Literally, the name, El Shaddai means 'the God who nourishes us at the breast'

It's as if two types of soul food are on offer, one is from God and nourishes us, the other leads only to destruction. The book of Revelation, chapter two, references this incident with Balaam, and promises, to those who overcome his deceptions, hidden manna from God, and fruit from the Tree of life - both pictures of spiritual nourishment. Similarly in Proverbs chapters eight and nine, wisdom and folly are depicted as two women calling passers-by to sit down and feast. We have a choice to make - an inner spiritual life sustained by God, or alternative spiritualities, which may look attractive, but in the end won't satisfy.

We must be careful as we get ready to launch out from lockdown not to get sidetracked, but to keep resetting our hearts; staying in that place of intimacy with Jesus, and finding our spiritual nourishment in Him alone.

CHAPTER NINE
COMING TO A FRESH START

God gives us a fresh start at things we might have felt beyond us the first time round. As we get ready for what is ahead, we have to trust that His timing is perfect and not get caught up in fear. He will lead us step by step. As we have ached for hugs from our children and grand children, God the Father's heart aches for His children to come home to Him.

The people of Israel had been there before, standing on the edge of the Promised land. Deuteronomy chapter one tells us that thirty-eight years before they had already been there, but through unbelief and rebellion they had been forced to turn back from its borders. Now they had finally returned. God had brought them back for a fresh start.

FEAR, OR FAITH?

On the previous occasion, they really had not been ready. They had been frightened of defeat by the Canaanites who lived there. They had sent out spies to report back about the land which God had promised them. When the spies returned, the people didn't really listen with faith to the good report about the land, given by two of the spies, Caleb and Joshua. Instead, they chose to believe the bad reports of the other ten spies, about the strength of the Canaanites and their fortified cities. Spying out the land had looked like a good idea, but it served to bring to the surface the condition of their hearts. Their choice was to listen with fear or with faith. With the noble exceptions of the two spies, Joshua and Caleb, the reaction of the people was one of fear.

GOD'S INSTRUCTIONS

'We will not launch out with God and take the land He has promised to give us' was their collective conclusion. They rebelled against His instruction, when He directed them to attack and take possession. You can sense Moses' frustration. They were almost there. *'Do not be terrified; do not be afraid of them,'* Moses said, *'The Lord your*

God who is going before you, will fight for you, as He did for you in Egypt before your very eyes, and in the desert' (Deut 1:29-31).

Then having refused these instructions, they rebelled again - not listening to God's next set of instructions to go back into the wilderness. Instead they had tried to pick up on His earlier command, to go forward and attack (Deut 1:43). Of course that didn't work out at all well for them! They were routed by the local inhabitants, who chased them off back into the desert, the very place where God had wanted them to go. They could have saved themselves such a lot of trouble if they'd listened up in the first place, and just gone!

We can only go forward as we listen to God's current instructions. If we fixate on something that's past its sell by date and try to follow that, we really confirm the rebellious state of our hearts. We must listen to the moment by moment instructions of the Holy Spirit, not how we think things ought to be. John 3:8 tells us that God's Spirit is like the wind whose movements are unpredictable. We really can't insist that God does things our way, as we get ready for our launch from lockdown.

A LACK OF TRUST IN GOD

The underlying heart issue of the people of Israel was their lack of trust in God. This had revealed itself in all its starkness when they had approached the land promised to them the first time.

Hear the madness of their words as they grumbled; *'The Lord hates us – He's brought us out to deliver us into the hands of the enemy to destroy us'* (Deut 1:27). *'Where can we go?'* they cried. But the only wise place to go was with God, to whatever and where ever He would lead them.

WALKING IN ANOTHER MAN'S SHOES

Let us put ourselves in their shoes for a moment – the people of Israel. God knew that it was going to need a whole generation spending time in the wilderness to bring about a change in them – a change in their attitude towards Him. Let us imagine that we are the people of Israel. Maybe this was the content of their conversation as they came to the end of their journey through the wilderness:- 'Every day seemed the same for us, nothing much happened, we woke up, we put on our shoes and packed up our tents and walked on through the dry landscape. But in the course of each day there were numerous opportunities to experience regret over our rebellious unbelief at the borders of the Promised Land. If only we had trusted God!

And so we have learnt that the journey through the wilderness has not been a waste of time, not for us, or for our parents. Every year of putting one foot in front of the other has been necessary, and has had a point. Each step in the process was sorting out our hearts, and making us ready to return to the difficult place where we had previously fluffed it. The shoes in which we have been walking, have sometimes been walking in the opposite geographical direction, but nevertheless each step was sure-footedly getting us back to the border of the Promised land. It has been necessary for us to take the scenic longer route in order for our hearts to be changed in their attitude towards God.

GROUNDHOG DAY!

In the film, Groundhog Day, the actor, Bill Murray plays a man who keeps waking up every day, to exactly the same day - Groundhog Day! We watched the film during the lockdown with our grown-up family, living in different areas. We counted down on a whatsapp group call, and pressed play simultaneously, so we could watch the movie together, and comment in a group chat on the funny bits, as the story unfolded. Although the man seemed to be locked into repeating the same day forever, at the beginning of each day, he always had a fresh start, and could choose how he might handle it.

By the end of the film, he had been on a character-changing journey for the better, and was finally released into the day after. When we look back on our experience during lockdown, may we find it to have been one of trusting in God, and one in which we have been changed; a journey where nothing will have been a waste of time. We may have needed lots of fresh starts as each day has unfolded, but God will have been in all of it.

A CHARACTER-CHANGING JOURNEY

The people of Israel again look back:- 'Over forty years in the wilderness, we have buried our parents and raised our children, and hopefully grown in wisdom. Finally, the last of the fighting men from the first generation out of Egypt has died, and his burial has been the trigger point for change just as God said it would be. The whole people have been waiting for one man to die!'

'We know that a new phase of our lives can now begin. We can set our compass northwards, to the Promised land. We have come back differently, and by a different route. It has taken us a long time, and we are not the same people as we once were. However, this is a good thing! We are ready for a fresh start.'

THE FATHER CARRIES US

Just like the people of Israel;, we are beginning to understand that it will be God's strength which will carry us successfully out of this wilderness. *'In the wilderness you saw how the Lord your God carried you as a father carries his son'* (Deut. 1:33). If we are fathers, we know all about carrying our children on our backs or in our arms. God has been behaving towards us as a loving father would. He has been carrying us every step of the way, bringing us through into a different place of the heart. A whole generation (and for us – the whole world!) has experienced the wilderness together, and are now ready to launch out.

'Everything has been just at the right time, appointed by God' (Psalm 75:2).

MISSING THE HUGS

One of the main things I have heard people saying, (including myself), that they have missed during lockdown, has been the physical contact- the hugs of children, friends, grandchildren etc. I have felt a huge ache sometimes, and even a bit of jealousy towards those who live close enough to go for a socially- distanced walk with a brother or sister, or chat to grandchildren from their garden. It has accentuated the 'empty nest' feeling that I have struggled with over the last few years, since all our children left home. God began to show me something, at that time, which helped me to cope. Here is a part of the poem I wrote about it:-

'Does God understand

How it feels to have an empty nest?

Does it help to know

He may feel it too?

When Adam and Eve left the garden

Do we remember His cry?

"Adam, Adam, where are you?"

When He hung on the cross,

Can we remember what He shouted out?

"My God, My God, why have You forsaken Me?

God is also a parent,

If His heart is breaking for His children

To come back home,

What does that mean for us?

Is there something we can learn from the 'empty nest'?

I think there is.

When you love, it hurts, and

We were made to live in Family;

Father is yearning,

Aching for His children

Like us, (or is it we, like Him?)

He misses them a lot!... *(from Empty Nest, Mary Bain, Feb 2018)*

COME HOME!

During this season of missing hugs from our family, we have been able to identify with God the Father's longing for His children to come back home to be with Him. Jesus illustrates this in the well-known story of the Prodigal son, in Luke chapter fifteen.

A father has two sons. One day the younger son asks his father for his share of the inheritance, and then leaves home. He travels to a far country and spends all his money, living it up with some so- called friends. When a famine hits that country, the son has nothing to eat, his friends are gone, and he can only get a job looking after pigs!

It is at this all time low point that he decides to return home, as we mentioned in the last chapter.

He wants to say sorry to his Father, and hopes that he will let him be one of his servants. In the meantime, the father has gone out every day, to a good view point looking for his son, and hoping he will see him coming home. On a certain day, he goes out to look as usual. In the far distance, he sees someone coming; 'Can it be him?' He is so excited he begins to run towards him. 'It is him!' He runs as fast as he can and when he reaches his son, he throws his arms around him as if he will never let go!

This is God our Father's heart for His children, who are away from Him. It is also the cry of our hearts! Many of us resonate with the metaphor of coming home to God. During this time of lockdown, God has been imprinting on our hearts this message. It is clear and simple - Father is looking for His children. Just as with the Israelites, He longs for us to trust Him, to come back to Him, to allow Him to carry us through the wilderness, and to give us a fresh new start in the Promised Land.

CARRY THE MESSAGE

One thing I felt God asking me to do personally, was to prepare a leaflet about His love, to give to some of the older people in the village. I gave the leaflet the title, WELCOME HOME, each letter in different colours. When Bob and I were involved in helping to deliver a weekly meal, to some of the elderly residents, I had the opportunity to pray with a couple of the ladies. They had been frightened about getting sick, or worried about a close friend. I began to realize that these ladies, and maybe others too, might appreciate something to read, to help them connect with God. I already knew about a book of prayers with lovely pictures, from an organization called The Prayer Trust, which was printed in large print, and I thought that my leaflet could be slipped inside this.

We have been able to give out several of these books and leaflets, and they have been received with thanks. One lady shared with me that she has prayed the prayer to ask Jesus into her life, and come home to her Heavenly Father (you can read this prayer on page 123 at the end of the book).

God, our Father is calling His children to come back home to Him. We know how He feels, the ache of His heart, because we have felt it too! As we come out after lockdown we can carry His message of love with us. There are people out there who need to hear it.

Deep Clean

Deep Clean

Clean up my heart, LORD
Like we are cleaning our kitchens,
Soaping our hands,
Clean me up, thoroughly,
Every bit of me, Lord!
Show me where the dirt still clings.
Cleanse me, purge me, till nothing remains
Of the vanity, the jealousy and all the stains
Left, on my conscience.
You may need some bleach,
Those hidden corners to reach!
But make me whiter than the snow
Whatever it takes, please do it;
My whole being is bowing low.
I know and respect You,
Repentance is serious stuff.
My hunger is pulling me deeper-
I cannot get enough;
I want to feel Your presence,
To know Your heart for all Your children;
In the cleansing and the breaking-
Take these pieces, LORD, and use me in Your kingdom.

Mary Bain   March 2020

PART THREE

LOOKING FORWARD

CHAPTER TEN
TROUBLE AHEAD

God is preparing us for what is ahead. Luke chapter twelve is like a warning road map, littered with reassurances of God's provision and protection but forecasting all kinds of trouble as well.

THE ROAD MAP

Our launch out of lockdown is not going to be trouble-free. Jesus warns us to always be watchful and ready for service (Luke 12:35-37). Lots of difficult things might be happening to us, but we are given at the same time, this wonderful promise by Jesus, *'Do not be afraid, little flock, for your Father has been pleased to give you the Kingdom'* (Luke 12:32).

In Luke chapter twelve, Jesus is warning his disciples about what they will encounter as they follow him. The whole chapter can be taken as a kind of prophetic road map, helping us to navigate what may lie ahead. The chapter culminates in teaching about the return of Christ for which the disciples are to be ready. *'The master...will come on a day when he does not expect him and at an hour he is not aware of'* (Luke 12:46). So similarly for us, the big answer to what is going to happen next, is the return of the Lord Jesus Christ! The long term plans we might have made, may get cut short after all. We cannot assume just because it hasn't happened yet, that it never will. Meanwhile, Jesus warned the first disciples of what lay immediately ahead for them – there would be crowds of people and religious Pharisees, and difficult issues with rulers and authorities. The twenty-first century equivalent of these groups are still around today.

THE CROWDS

The ministry of Jesus was characterised by large crowds. He was *'preaching the good news of the Kingdom, and healing every disease and sickness among the people. News about him spread all over Syria....large crowds...followed him'* (Matthew 4:23-25). At the start of Luke chapter twelve, *'a crowd of many thousands had gathered, so that they were trampling on one another'* (Luke 12:1).

This was also the experience of the first disciples later. It wasn't just something special that Jesus experienced. For example, when Philip went down to a city called Samaria, large crowds gathered to listen to him and to see the miraculous signs he did. He was healing the sick and the whole city was affected. *'There was great joy in that city'* (see Acts 8:4-7). Philip's preaching of the gospel and the healing miracles that followed were an atmosphere changer. The overall effect on the community was to take it to a place of great joy.

Jesus response to seeing the great crowds that were coming out to hear him was one of compassion. He felt they were harassed and helpless like sheep without a shepherd. He also saw the crowd as an abundant harvest, ready to be reaped (John 4:35). His prayer was to ask the Lord of the harvest to send out workers into his harvest field (Matthew 9:35-38). The disciples became their own answered prayer when Jesus then sends them out to preach that the Kingdom of Heaven is near (see Matthew chapter ten, a passage which parallels Luke chapter twelve in much of its content).

What will the crowds look like in our own context? Will we respond towards them with compassion? Will there be any crowds at all in a climate conditioned by months of physical distancing? In any case, there may not be the ability to hold mass gatherings for several months. We anticipate a continuing general reluctance for people to go near one another for a while, even if there is no legislation to prevent them. Habit patterns formed by caution and fear will not go away immediately.

CHURCH ONLINE

However, crowds are going to be around, but in a different way, expressed in a level of participation in online gospel events unheard of beforehand. The ice has already been broken with evidence coming in from a UK Tearfund survey, for example, that over twenty-four per cent of the nation have newly tuned into online church services in the lockdown period. The normal percentage was five to seven per cent attending one church service per month. Personal stories of coming to know Jesus and being healed through prayer will be out there on Facebook and other platforms. A critical threshold will be reached where mainstream media will pick up on this and further fuel the interest. News will spread and the numbers being impacted will rise even more dramatically. There may not be physical crowds trampling on one another but a dramatic change in numbers identifying themselves as Christians is coming. Now there's a prediction to ponder on! If we're right, then there will need to be a gear-shift in how churches respond in receiving them. A good exercise to think through either way. If we're wrong, like the prophet, Habakkuk, we will praise God anyway.

'Though the fig tree does not bud and there are no grapes on the vines…yet I will rejoice in the Lord. I will be joyful in God my Saviour' (Hab. 3:17-18).

PUSHBACK

Not everyone will be happy with this good news. A spike in numbers of people publicly acknowledging the impact of Jesus in their lives, will be seen by some as a threat. Counter ideologies, which have worked against the influence of the gospel in our society for years, will pushback, sensing that the territory they have got used to holding, might be overwhelmed. This sudden blossoming of interest in Jesus will be smeared as dangerous. At first it will be portrayed as marginal and ridiculous, and will not be taken seriously by its adversaries. Then as the numbers affected increases, social distancing from it will be advised. Critics will label it as populist, simplistic and even call it extremism. Attempts will be made to shut down its online presence and undermine its validity.

Just before the teaching in Luke chapter twelve, Jesus had had a major confrontation with the Pharisees and the teachers of the law – the religious leaders of his day. In a series of six 'woes', he describes them as greedy, wicked and foolish. Finally he says, *'Woe to you experts in the law, because you have taken away the key to knowledge. You yourselves have not entered, and you have hindered those who were entering'* (Luke 11:52). It is hardly surprising that Luke's gospel records, *'The Pharisees and the teachers of the law began to oppose him fiercely and to besiege him with questions, waiting to catch him in something he might say'* (Luke 11:53-54).

Jesus had shown them up and he was not welcome. They were insulted and offended but eventually, Matthew's gospel tells us, that they handed Jesus over to be crucified for another reason. They were motivated by jealousy (Matthew 27:18). Jesus was outshining them and they felt their position in society was being undermined. If crowds were following Jesus, then they weren't following them!

Sadly, there will be elements in society today which have previously enjoyed a sense of privilege and entitlement, who will react badly to the changing spiritual landscape. We can expect, for example, to be besieged, like Jesus, by questions from people whose intention is to catch us out in some way. We may even find ourselves in legal proceedings. Lord, have mercy on us! Who wants that? About this possibility, Jesus gave these reassuring words to his first disciples in Luke chapter twelve, and they are a reassurance for us as well. *'Don't worry about how you will defend yourselves or what you will say', says Jesus, 'for the Holy Spirit will teach you at that time what you should say'* (Luke 12:11-12). This level of pushback will not be unexpected.

INHERITANCE SQUABBLES

Someone in the crowd asked Jesus to sort out a family inheritance issue (Luke 12:13). Jesus used the occasion to warn everyone to *'Watch out! Be on your guard against all kinds of greed; a man's life does not consist in the abundance of his possessions'* (Luke 12:15). So what is our inheritance that we might find ourselves squabbling over with others? I think there is a spiritual dimension to what constitutes our inheritance, which we need to be aware of beyond the material. Each of us has been given unique things to do in life. There are territories to function within, which we can understand to be ours, which aren't just on the material or human level. They have a spiritual dimension to them as well. The apostle Paul wrote in the context of church mission about himself and others, that they were *'only servants, through who you came to believe, as the Lord has assigned to each his task'* (1 Corinthian 3:5). We will be rewarded to the extent of our faithfulness to the tasks each one of us has been given by God.

The Corinthian church, for example, were squabbling and forming divisions around different personalities. We can expect to see similar spiritual inheritance squabbles flaring up at this time of change as well. Brothers and sisters in Christ who are determined to argue over what things belong to who. We need to take a lesson from the apostle Paul, for example, who was very careful to operate within the territory God had assigned him, and no further. Ahead of us, there are assignments for each of us to do. We need to beware of all kinds of greed. If we pick up spiritual assignments that are not ours, we go beyond our capacity, and are effectively being greedy. It is always sad when one sees churches operating as if they are the last and only word on mission in an area. The mission field is great and yet they want to insist that the whole task is done by only themselves. To paraphrase the statement from the globally influential Lausanne Movement, about reaching the whole world with the gospel message – 'It takes the whole church to reach the whole community with the gospel' (Lausanne.org).

FAMILY DIVISIONS

Jesus warned his first disciples to expect family divisions. He asked them a rhetorical question, *'Do you think I came to bring peace on earth? No, I tell you but division. From now on, there will be five in one family, divided against each other, three against two and two against three'* (Luke 12:52). What a shocking answer! When people believe in Jesus, it brings a dividing of the ways regarding behaviour. Some family members may think it strange that a new Christian, or one who has chosen to recommit their life to God, will no longer plunge with them into the kinds of behaviour they used to do (1 Peter 4:4). Actually it can also work the other way round, when some clean-living older brother, for example, finds it hard to accept that a wayward family member has now changed but instead is determined never to forgive them for their messed-up past (see the parable of the two sons in Luke 15:11-32).

Jesus' warnings in Luke chapter twelve indicate that there is plenty of trouble ahead for all who follow him. If we are aware of this, we can pray that God will help us, and that there will be good relationships between Christians, and that our families will be preserved from being ripped apart by argument and tensions. You may already be in difficult family circumstances in which case, it is time to cry out to God for reconciliation between yourself and family members.

'If it is possible, as far as it depends on you, live at peace with everyone' (Romans 12:18).

'How good and pleasant it is when brothers live together in unity...for there the Lord bestows his blessing' (see Psalm 133)

GOD WILL PROVIDE

However, whatever the future, Jesus told the disciples that God would provide. They are not to be afraid and not to worry. They are much more valuable than the birds. Their Heavenly Father would give them their food and clothes. Luke chapter twelve is full of reassurances from Jesus that God will protect and provide for them. *'Not one sparrow is forgotten by God. Indeed the very hairs of your head are numbered. Don't be afraid, you are worth more than many sparrows'* (Luke 12:7). This teaching is for us too – God is with us and will provide for us in whatever lies ahead.

At the start of the lockdown, there was a rush to get down to the supermarkets before everything ran out. When we got down there the place was heaving. It felt like the Christmas season had started early. However, instead of luxuries, people were loading all sorts of necessities into their trolleys. The canned meat shelves, for example were completely empty. Hopefully, we learnt that there really wasn't any point in buying ten years worth of loo roll? But who bought all those packets of Chicken Kiev? I mention Chicken Kiev because I don't even like it, but I remember seeing a packet of the stuff among the few frozen items left in the shop, and thinking should I buy it just in case! How ridiculous can you get! Thankfully, I didn't buy it. Jesus tells us that we should be rich towards God and seek first His kingdom (Luke 12:21, 31), and not to be fearful or greedy. We need to trust that God is looking after us.

'Man shall not live on bread alone but by every word that proceeds from the mouth of God' (Matt 4:4). The nourishment we receive from God's words sustains our inner beings. He is our bread of life and the great lover of our souls. When we draw near to him, and

spend time in His presence, we are fed and truly satisfied at every level, materially, as well as spiritually.

Similarly, Jesus reassured the first disciples about their clothes. He told them that the lilies of the field were covered in splendour – more so than that of King Solomon, but that they were much more covered in God's splendour than either the lilies or Solomon (Luke 12:27-28). We, also, don't need to worry about our clothes, or how God chooses to display His spiritual beauty in us. He has our clothes all sorted!

The next big fixture is the return of Jesus. He has promised this is in our diaries in invisible ink on an unknown date. It will happen but when we least expect it! When Jesus does return, Luke chapter twelve tells us that he wants to find us in position, doing what we know we should be doing. The disciples are to be watchful – to be dressed ready for service and to keep their lamps burning (Luke 12:35).

As we come out of lockdown, let's keep an eye on the road map Jesus has given us in Luke chapter twelve, with its warnings and promises of God's provision.

'The Son of Man will come at an hour when you do not expect him' (Luke 12:40).

'From everyone who has been given much, much will be demanded; and from the one who has been entrusted with much, much more will be asked' (Luke 12:48).

CHAPTER ELEVEN
PREPARATIONS

There are preparations to make as we launch out from the lockdown. We need to take stock and get organised for what's ahead. It's important to be ourselves, to foster our family relationships and celebrate the journey so far.

TAKING STOCK

As we launch out of lockdown, we need to do a stock check on our resources. What is in our tool kit for what's ahead? Someone we know, described it as their arsenal. They were getting things ready for battle, and polishing up their armour.

For example, we have been sorting out things in the prayer garden. Two years on from our launch celebration, some of the things need replacing and sorting out. We have a 'Narnia' wardrobe, for example, hidden behind the summerhouse, which one can walk through into another part of the garden. It was looking a bit worse for wear and we have now upgraded it. We are creating a plant file so we can understand better how to look after the plants in the garden. We've ordered new metal butterflies to add to the ones on our outside, 'River of Life' mural.

Proverbs chapter twenty-seven tells us to *'be sure to know the condition of your flocks; to give careful attention to your herds'.* When we do this, there is a promise of a good harvest and provision, not just for ourselves, but for everyone associated with us. (Proverbs 27:23-27). We have work to do which will bless all of us, and the land itself, when we do it. God promises to give us all the wisdom we need. James 1:5 tells us, *'If any of you lack wisdom, he should ask God, who gives generously to all without finding fault, and it will be given him.'*

God cares for the earth and wants to bless our stewardship over it. Psalm sixty-five says about God, *'You care for the land and water it; you enrich it abundantly. The streams of God are filled with water to provide the people with corn, for so you have ordained it... The meadows are covered with flocks and the valleys are mantled with corn; they shout for joy and sing'* (Psalm 65:9-13).

USING WHAT WE HAVE

'What have you got in your hand?' God asks Moses this question by a burning bush in the wilderness (Exodus 4:2). God had caught his attention through this strange sight and then speaks to him from within the bush. He wants him to lead the people of Israel out of Egypt, but Moses doesn't feel up to the job, and makes a series of excuses for why God should send someone else. When God asks the question, Moses replies that he has his staff in his hand – an ordinary work-a-day staff that he would use to look after his sheep, and protect them if there was danger. It didn't look like much to offer, but God was interested in what Moses had, not in what he didn't have. Then supernaturally, in God's power, Moses goes on to do far more with that staff than we would ever have imagined! Later, when Moses raised his staff, for example, the Red sea parted and all the people of Israel walked through on dry land out of Egypt (Exodus 14:16).

At one point in Jesus' ministry, he had gone away privately to a solitary place to get some rest (Mark 6:31). But a large crowd found out where he was, and followed him there. It was a remote place and as the day grew late the logistics of where they would all get food was pressing on the disciples' thinking. Jesus asked them a similar question to the one God had asked Moses, 'How many loaves do you have? In other words what have you got to hand? Then one of the disciples called Andrew pipes up, *'Here is a boy with five small barley loaves and two small fish, but how far will they go among so many?'* The small boy had given to Jesus what he had in his hand. It didn't appear to amount to much, but after Jesus had prayed over the food, and blessed it, it became a meal which fed five thousand men (John 6:5-13). How amazing is that?

As an old song goes, 'Little becomes much when we place it in the Master's hands'. We may feel we haven't much to offer Jesus, but he is pleased when we give all that we are to him, whatever we think of ourselves. It is a useful exercise to write down what you enjoy doing, and the skills you have developed over the years. When you look at the list, the things written there may not seem much to you, but when given willingly to Jesus, he is able to do amazing things.

BEING OURSELVES

We are uniquely who we are. We cannot be someone else, but we carry our own calling and destiny. So we are not to be jealous of what is going on in other people's lives. And we should not be hypocritical, and pretend to be someone we are not. God loves the person He made each of us to be, and doesn't want any fake versions! Paul writes in Romans chapter twelve, *'Do not think of yourself more highly than you ought, but rather think of yourself with sober judgment in accordance with the measure of faith God has given you'* (Romans 12:3). He then goes on to say that *'We have different gifts, according to the grace given us'* (Romans 12:6).

If you have never done a personality test, there are some free ones online which can be illuminating, and help us to discover more about who we are. What do <u>we</u> like doing? Let's not pretend we like something if we don't, but instead flow with who we are.

GETTING ORGANISED

We have to organise ourselves to increase our capacity for what may be ahead. A big harvest of people coming to know Jesus will need resources. There will be people, of whom we may be aware, who can help us to do our work better. For example, in the wilderness Moses was getting overworked, and was hearing all the problems different people were having with one another, every hour of the day. He realized he needed to set up a judiciary, so that he didn't have to spend all his time hearing disputes (Deut. 1:10). Moses had reached his personal capacity to handle what was going on. If he hadn't changed how he was organizing his life, it would have seriously affected his ability to lead. He was facing a mission impossible, and could have decided to quit. But that would have contradicted all that God had led him through, up to that point. He found a solution which involved other people helping him. Similarly, we mustn't let our personal capacity limit the plans we believe God has for us. We mustn't say, 'Enough is enough – No more!' The prayer of Moses was an expansive one – *'May the Lord the God of your fathers increase you a thousand times and bless you as the Lord has promised'* (Deut. 1:11). It is ok to recognise that some things may be beyond our competence, and seek help from those who have greater competence. There is always a way through to a solution, even if at first, it looks like we are heading towards a dead-end brick wall!

A good idea, in getting organised, may be to write down the people who may be able to help us, and then those who we might be able to help in return. God is interested in helping us; in the details of our planning, as well as the bigger things in life. He can show us who we might need to partner with, or call on. During the lockdown, Mary and I have spent some time brainstorming some of the things that we think may be ahead for us, in the coming months. We may not get everything right, but it helps to aim to get organised for the year ahead, and to think about the people who may be in it. We have been quite nervous about leaving the habit patterns and routines we have developed over the lockdown period, and strangely, a bit of us would have liked them to have gone on indefinitely. It shows how quickly one can get institutionalized! The months ahead look manic, as we know we will be on catch-up, with stuff that we were unable to do before, and now really must address. We don't want to lose sight of the steady routines which we felt have been good for us – the daily exercise, for example, and the zoom calls with family members scattered around the country, and one son and his family, even in Australia. But we understand that we will be in a different season and need to be organized for it. Having said that, there may be some things we were doing previous to the lockdown, that it is now time to say goodbye to, so it could be useful to consider what these might be as w

FA   ATIONSHIPS

The   s increased the communications in our family. Bes   r zoom chats, we have also played games and wat   all via the internet. We have taken it in turns to cre   iz, and even had some prayer and sharing times. Go   oster the family relationships we have, and not take the   In changed circumstances, we will want to ensure tha   relationships, which we have developed don't de

So   ations may be extremely difficult, and we need to be   get intimidated, or upset, by the lack of warmth wh   displayed towards us, by others. Someone once pr   have a tougher skin and a tender heart. It may be,   dly behaviour on our part, consistently given, will   t the ice within our family. At the very least, it is a   ray for your family members on a regular basis. Dig   off some photos, to remind you to pray for them.

e of Israel approached the river Jordan and their launch into the Promised land, they had to go through areas occupied by distant family relatives, who had already settled there. These were descendants of Esau, the brother of their ancestor Jacob, and of Lot, who was a cousin. God warned the people of Israel to be very careful in how they behaved with their family relatives. They were to pass through their lands peacefully, and if stopped, they were to respect their boundaries, and skirt around them, to get to the river Jordan (see Deuteronomy chapter 2). From their experience, we may need to learn something about how to behave towards our own family and relatives. People have their own ways to go in life, so we should respect that, stay supportive, and allow them space to be who they are.

REMEMBER THE JOURNEY - KEEP A JOURNAL

It is always encouraging when we remember and celebrate where we have come from, the experiences on the way, and the Lord's presence with us, in it all. Moses helps the people of Israel to remember what they've been through in his speech (see Deuteronomy chapters 1 to 3). He reminds them of the highlights of forty years together, from that first moment of deliverance out of slavery in Egypt. Elsewhere, in the book of Numbers, Moses got a lot more detailed in his descriptions. He records there, for example, every place where they camped! Moses had basically kept a journal, all the way through their journey in the wilderness.

It's not too late to sit down and think through the highlights of our particular lockdown experience. It is a great habit, at any time, to write down the things that go on in your life. Moses, in Psalm ninety, says, *'Teach us to number our days aright, that we may gain a heart of wisdom'* (Ps.90:12). Keeping a regular journal of what God has been doing in your life, and recording the highlights of each week, and the people you meet, helps you remember and celebrate God's goodness towards you.

The prophet Micah tells us to remember the journey that we have been on (see Micah chapter six). He lists some of the highlights. Micah, like Moses, starts with their rescue as a nation from Egypt. Similarly, we want to celebrate God's goodness in rescuing us from sin. This is the most incredible, wonderful thing to have ever happened to us. However, there are some other things on his list which are a surprise. Balaam's failure to curse Israel, for example, which we mentioned earlier in chapter eight, is also on his list. Micah wanted them to remember that even Israel's enemies could only bless her! Incredible! God has spread a table before us in the presence of our enemies, says David, in Psalm twenty-three. Let us remember that God's provision and protection have been with us all the way through our lives. Unfortunately, we are too good at forgetting the things that God has done for us. Keeping a journal helps us to remember, and celebrate with thankfulness and appreciation.

CHAPTER TWELVE
WHAT NEXT?

The following are words and visions, which I believe are from God (you can make your own assessment!) for whatever is next on His agenda for us.

We believe that these words and visions are relevant to us personally, and for the church, or however we see things beyond the 'me and mine' of our daily living. Your imagination may want to re-imagine these words and pictures, inside your own head. It is surprising, and a wonder, how most of us can do this! The first picture is actually on the front cover of the book, so you will need to go there to imagine that one!

As you unpack the pictures and words, and consider them, pray that God will give you something – an understanding that will help in your context.

Focus on what God may be saying especially to you, and pray about the 'what next?' He has for you.

You will probably need a bit of time to reflect on each section in turn. I suggest that you don't rush through. However, you may want to get a quick overview, and then go back through in a more considered way afterwards.

Another approach might be for you to flick through the pictures, and then pick out one or two in particular, which have resonated with you. You may want to write something down.

The words and pictures are intended to stir up new ways of looking at your situation and, later on, they may speak to you in different ways again. Some of the pictures may disturb you – let them. Others may leave you unmoved – they may not be needed at this moment. In picture form, here is what we see coming up in this launching out period. There are eight sections in all.

A PLANE AND A ROCK – SAFETY

I saw <u>a plane taking off</u> from a runway, behind which was a wall of fire. I saw <u>a rock, with waves surging around it</u>, and I heard God's reassuring words that we would be safe; we are safe in the plane taking off, and safe on the rock, though all around us, spectacular, God-orchestrated things are happening. There is a take off, and a dramatic growth. We have had something to do with the fact that there is a wall of fire, erupting behind us.

A COILED ROPE AND AN OPEN BOOK – STORY

I saw <u>a coiled rope.</u> At first it looked like a tangle, but in fact there was an order, a pattern and a beauty in it. There were a lot of strands, because there are still a lot of things to come.

I saw <u>an open book</u>, the words of which I couldn't make out, but the story continues, and there is a good plan ahead.

We have a hope and a future. The full story hasn't been written yet, but on the open page, <u>one word is visible – grandmother</u>. The Lord is turning our hearts to connect across the generations. The grandmothers will turn a generation to the Lord.

[Notes:'He [Elijah] will turn the hearts of the fathers to their children, and the hearts of the children to their fathers...'
(Malachi 4:6).]

A BOWL AND A TOWEL – SERVICE

I saw <u>a bowl and a towel</u>. The church after lockdown will be a church that serves, by washing the feet of those who have newly entered. The question will be asked to the people coming in, 'How can we serve you?' Not, 'How can you serve us?' The five-fold gifts, described in Ephesians 4:11, will finally parent the church into full maturity.

[Notes: These gifts of apostle, prophet, evangelist, pastor and teacher are present in the church, for the equipping of God's people for works of service, so that we might all mature into *the whole measure of the fullness of Christ'* (Ephesians 4:13).
Jesus washed the feet of the first disciples as a servant to set them an example (John 13:1-17).]

A KALEIDOSCOPE - SHAKEN

I saw a Kaleidoscope. The old frames of reference have been shaken, and there is a new kaleidoscope of patterns, which in turn, are being shaken, and shaken again, and there is a beauty and a prettiness in this.

BRENDAN AND BRIGID – MOVEMENT

Brendans will travel, and Brigids will receive. Brendan and Brigid were Celtic saints – Brendan was known as Brendan the Voyager, and Brigid was known for her hospitality to passing strangers. There will be a lot more movement, as people discover different ways of being church. This is glory on legs - the glory of a church on the move! I believe the church after lockdown will have a new dynamic, and fluidity about it. Brendan and Brigid types will be prevalent, and minister to people by divine appointment – encounters in a passing moment.

AN AXE AND AN ARROW - READINESS
I saw an axe being sharpened, and an arrow being fired. We are being prepared for specific and precise assignments.

TAMAR SITTING BY THE WAYSIDE

I saw Tamar sitting by a roadside, and a righteous resolution and restoration of proper relationships in the house. No longer would gifting be left in limbo, abused and out of place. Her father-in-law had left her hanging (see Genesis 38) but there will be resolution.

The barren fig tree has been 'digged and dunged' and fruit is expected (Luke 13:6-8). The baby will be born to Tamar.

[Notes: there are some thoughts on Tamar in the appendix]

A SONG OF INTIMACY

I saw a deepening of intimacy, a song of intimacy, and a garden of prayer. We are back in the garden.

'Therefore the redeemed of the Lord shall return and come with singing unto Zion, and everlasting joy shall be upon their heads. They shall obtain gladness and joy, and sorrow shall flee away' (Isaiah 35:10, 51:11).

[Note: the garden is the Paradise of God where He walks with us]

CHAPTER THIRTEEN
A JOURNEY INTO INTIMACY

The lockdown has felt like a Preparation time in many ways for us. The Bridegroom has been calling us into the secret place of intimacy, to fall in love with Him again!

FALLING IN LOVE AGAIN

I entered into the Lockdown having already begun a Lent Challenge that the Bible Society had set up. This involved memorizing a bible verse each day, from a list which they had compiled. The idea was that for every day in Lent (except Sundays), you memorized the verse/verses and then took a video of yourself, which you shared on Facebook, and tagged one friend to challenge them to also take up the Lent challenge! The challenge was very good for me! I soon realized that in order to learn the verse, I had to really understand what God was speaking to me through it. I could not memorise it by rote, and then share it with any passion, if I hadn't spent time taking in the message myself. Learning the verses became the main content of my time with God each day, and started to have a big effect upon me.

Many of the verses chosen by the Bible Society were foundational ones, for example, John 3:16.
'For God so loved the world that He gave His only Son that whoever believes in Him should not perish but have eternal life'.

Several were ones that I had learnt, just after I gave my life to Jesus, when I was a university student. I felt as if God was reminding me of the basics of my faith, and drawing me back, to remember that time of first falling in love with Him.
(If you would like to see some of my Lent Challenge posts, there are a few posted on our Facebook ministry page, Welcome Network, as well as on my profile page).

I wrote the following poem a few years ago, when we were moving house. It expresses something of how I came to meet Jesus; the excitement and the wonder I felt when I gave my life to him. During the lockdown, Bob and I facilitated a global zoom call entitled 'Back to First Love', to our network of friends around the world. It was an amazing experience, as people joined us from as far away as Tahiti and Taiwan! I read out this poem to introduce the session. It helped participants to consider their own feelings when they first came to know Jesus.

The Invitation

I found it a few days ago

Sorting out things for the move

I had forgotten how big it was

Edged in gold

White card, hand written

Beautiful, carefully crafted,

My personal invitation-

To the Wedding.

Wrapped around it, even still

The soft tissue paper

I had kept, as it had been then,

Covered in hearts, and still carrying

The sweet, lingering perfume

Of His presence...

I pulled it off

And held the card in my hand...

The years rolled away

I was a student again

Sitting on my bed,

A Sunday evening after Mass,
Alone.
My heart aching within me
I had been learning something hard to handle,
It made me feel lonely and afraid,
The man I thought was in love with me
Wanted me to be someone else.

The scene moved forward;
I was drinking coffee
In Bob's new room,
Chatting and laughing,
Feeling excited again
My heart beating fast
As our eyes met and we shared
About the book
He'd been reading that week
Could it really be true?

Then, another scene;
A conversation with Bob's friend, a Christian,
"Did I really know Jesus?" was the question;
"Did I know what He had done for me?"
I thought I did;
I answered all the questions correctly,
Except the last.
Why had no one said this before?
"Had I really given Him my heart?"

Back in my own room again
I read through the leaflet
Bob's friend had given me
It made such perfect sense;
Every word spoke hope and healing
Into my empty, aching heart.
I had been looking for a man
To fill the void inside,
Give me affirmation,
To love me, just as I am.
I discovered Jesus,
Loving me completely, totally,
Even before I was born!
Dying, just for me;
It went far and beyond the love of a man!
Nothing more was needed;
I prayed a simple prayer
And opened my heart to Him...

And that was when I received the Invitation;
As I slept that night,
Jesus walked into my room.
I felt His presence,
His touch on my forehead,
His soft whisper of love,
"Now you are Mine."
In the morning I found the card
On my pillow,

My name written at the top
In gold, and below
Three simple words-
"Come, follow Me!"

And so the Invitation is definitely being packed
With all our belongings
As Bob and I move on today.
The joy found in following Jesus
Continues to grow.
And I know
It was the best decision I have ever made
To give my heart, and live my life,
Forever, with Him.

And yes, the Wedding is still to come,
And the Bridegroom is tenderly calling
To you, dear Reader;
Have you discovered your invitation yet?
He is waiting for you.

Mary Bain April 2017

(The physical wedding invitation card, referred to in the poem, is poetic license, but the meeting I describe with Jesus really happened)

Mary.

Together with His Father and the Holy Spirit,
The Bridegroom, Jesus Christ & His lovely Bride,
the Church,
Request the honour of your presence
at their WEDDING...

"COME
FOLLOW
ME!"

and afterwards
at the Marriage Supper of the LAMB.

RSVP

CHAPTER FOURTEEN
THE WEDDING

The desire of the Bridegroom is for us to open our hearts fully to him, and to know him as we have never known him before!

THE BRIDEGROOM IS SINGING OVER US

In Hosea Chapter 2:14-16, as we have already read in Chapter 8, the Lord leads his Prodigal wife into the wilderness, in order to regain her first love. He does this out of his love for her, wooing her and speaking tenderly to her. We have felt the call of our Bridegroom, Jesus, during this time, calling us into a deeper intimacy with him.
He promises to his Bride, *'I will betroth you to me forever; ...and in that day I will sing, declares the LORD.'* Hosea 2:19-21

The imagery of the Wedding has been with us since the beginning of time. Since God fashioned the first woman, taking her out of Adam's side. It has always seemed quite wonderful to me that the closeness, the union that God desires for us to experience, is imaged in the union between a husband and wife.
There is a wedding to come, described as the Marriage supper of the Lamb and the Invitation has been sent out to all who will receive it!

THE YEAR OF WEDDINGS

Bob and I have a large family- seven children to be exact! In 2016 both our eldest son and our eldest daughter chose to get married. We were thrilled! But as well as these two weddings, three of their cousins were also married in the same year! We called it 'The Year of Weddings'! God began to talk to us on the theme of weddings a lot that year. I got particularly focused on what God was saying, because I had been asked, by my daughter to share a prayer at her wedding, and by my son to write a poem.

I had been reading in the Song of Songs, and also studying John chapter two, about the wedding at Cana. But then I began to think about the theme of the Bride and the Bridegroom which runs through the whole Bible.

The poem I wrote was not the one I read out at the wedding, as it was too long! I wrote a shorter one instead.

However, my original poem does convey the joy of the relationship that God desires each one of us to experience, forever with Him. Can you hear the melody of His Love song?

A WEDDING SONG

Love's Beginning

It all begins in a garden

A garden full of life and colour

Bursting with brilliance and light

Scents and smells

Goodness and fruitfulness

Filled with a peaceful Presence

And bringing purpose and order,

In the care and keeping of it.

And in the garden, a man who is lonely.

No bird or animal can fill the gap within his heart

Although many are brought to him

And he gives names to them all.

Until a marvelous miracle occurs

A part of him is taken, while he sleeps

And when he awakes

He finds standing before him

The most beautiful creature of all-

A woman, who just fills and completes his life.

And the wedding bells ring out for the first time,

As two become one in marriage!

Love's Song

Today, let's listen to their love song,

The Bridegroom is singing it now

and has been throughout the years.

We can just catch the strains of the melody-

'*Come away with me*' he sings

'My beautiful one,

All of me loves all of you,

All your curves and all your edges

All your perfect imperfections...

Don't go changing to try to please me

Girl, you're amazing,

Just the way you are!'

And now the bride joins in,

'Blow upon my garden of spices my lover,

Je t'aime...

Your gentleness has captured my heart,

I give my all to you....'

Love's Future

Looking forward into the future-

A new beginning, a city shining with light.

Here is the Bridegroom,

Wooing each one of us to Himself.

He is full of love for His beautiful bride.

Constant and faithful,

Choosing only to see the best in her.

She has made herself ready,

And is longing to be with Him.

The invitations are sent to everyone,

No one is forgotten.

A magnificent banquet is laid out

And the Bridegroom and His bride are calling,

'Come and drink!'

The wine is flowing in a never-ending stream

And there is a place for each of us at the table.

Let's choose to take part, and enter in

As the wedding bells ring with joy

And two <u>forever </u>become One in marriage.

Mary Bain   April 2016

(Some of the words in the middle section are from 'All of Me' by Jasmine Thompson, sung by John Legend, and 'Just The Way You Are' by Bruno Mars which were popular songs in the Bain household at the time!)

A prophetic word given to me a few years ago, expresses the intimacy into which Jesus is calling us. "Dance with me, my darling, my love! I love you! Dance with me...I want to swirl you and twirl you and I want to whisper in your ears my words of love. I am your Lover and Your Lord. Dance with me!"

Wow! How wonderful it felt for me to hear and receive these words of love!

PREPARING FOR THE WEDDING

'Let us rejoice and be glad; let us praise His greatness! For the time has come for the wedding of the Lamb, and His bride has prepared herself for it' Revelation 19:7

Have we heard God challenging us during the time of lockdown? We certainly felt Him asking us how we were going to use the extra time that had been freed up. There is always a choice whether we will spend time drawing close to God, or whether we will fill our days with other things. Many times during the lockdown, we have had to make this choice. I found the more settled routine that we had developed at home, really helped me to fit a daily time with God into my schedule. Prior to this, our pattern of working involved a lot of travelling, which meant that it was difficult to always meet with God at a regular time. But when you are in love with someone, don't you want to spend every moment with them? Yes, but this doesn't mean that you don't get on with the necessities of daily living – eating, sleeping, working, relaxing etc., but that you do these things together with the one you love. Jesus, your Lover, is walking with you throughout your day.

SOME WAYS OF DRAWING CLOSER TO JESUS

It is good to spend some focused time each day in God's presence. It is during this time that we can hear His voice more clearly, encounter His presence and be refreshed, and restored by the Holy Spirit. This is how we can prepare ourselves to launch out as His Bride, and enjoy His love in this new season. Below are some ways I have found helpful in drawing closer to God.

- Give your day to Jesus when you first wake up. Use the Our Father Prayer.

- Spend time in worship- singing, dancing, drawing, painting, gardening!

- Sit quietly, giving your heart to Him, being still.

- When you read the Bible, focus on a Bible story and imagine you are one of the characters in it. Think about your feelings, what questions you might ask Jesus, what you are seeing, hearing smelling etc. What is God saying to you? Write or draw to express yourself.

- In your Bible reading, pick out one verse that speaks to you. Write it out, carry it with you, memorise it and ponder on it during your day.

- Read aloud a short section of the Bible. As you read listen to the words. Are there phrases that stick out for you? Pause and think about them. Read the passage again slowly. What is God speaking into your heart? Write or draw it.

- Use different postures to help you as you pray and listen to God- kneeling, standing, lying on your face etc. One posture I have found helpful is lying on my back with arms outstretched and giving my whole self to Him. It is a vulnerable posture, in which you can give God access to your inner being- giving and also receiving His love.

- Write out or draw your prayers. Later, you can look back and see answers!

- Think of three things to thank God for at the end of the day.

- Have a set time which you try to keep each day with God, but if it gets disrupted, even spending a few moments giving your heart to Him or looking at a few verses in your Bible is better than doing nothing! Remember that he loves you and His heart is always towards you.

Our imaginations have been given to us, as a wonderful gift from God. We are seeing a release of creativity in this season, in many different forms, which is wonderful to behold. We reflect the nature of God, our Creator, when we begin to step out in expressing the creativity that He has put within us. e.g. in art, music, singing, poetry, dancing, cooking etc. We can also use our imaginations in our encounters with Jesus.

UNDER THE VEIL

Imagine it is your wedding day, you are standing face to face with your darling, foreheads touching, so close you can smell their perfume, the spices in their aftershave; there is a glow in your cheeks and a huge smile on your face, and you are looking into one another's eyes. It is as if time is standing still...

Listen, your darling is speaking:-

"My beloved spoke, and said to me;

Rise up, my love, my fair one,

And come away.

For lo, the winter is past,

The rain is over and gone,

The flowers appear on the earth;

The time of singing has come,

And the voice of the turtledove

Is heard in our land.

The fig tree puts forth her green figs,

And the vines with the tender grapes

Give a good smell,

Rise up, my love, my fair one,

And come away!'   (Song of Songs 2:10-13)

Jesus, our Bridegroom, wants to speak tenderly to His Bride, to encourage us, and to show us His love. A new season has come, there is fruitfulness ahead. We can rise up; we are His fair one and He is calling us out into a new phase of life after lockdown.

Let's be prepared and ready to go out, together with Him!

No Limit Love

No Limit Love

Your Love has no boundaries
It just keeps on
Giving, extending, reaching out
Further and further
Encompassing all;
Stretching out the tent pegs,
No limits
Overwhelming, Never-ending
V   a   s   t
H   U   G   E
E   x   t   e   n   s   i   v   e
Amazing and wonderful!
No boundaries and no end
Your Love expands and expands and expands
Forever and ever
AMEN.

Mary Bain March 2020

A PRAYER to ask Jesus to come into my life

Dear God,

THANK YOU that You love me, and that there is a home in Heaven for me. Thank you Jesus, that You took the blame for my sin and died for me.

I am **SORRY** for living only for myself, for hurting You and the people around me.

PLEASE forgive me for everything I have done wrong and come into my life.

TODAY, I am coming Home!

I choose to put my trust in You, Jesus, and from now on,

I want to live my life only for You. **AMEN.**

If you prayed this prayer let us know, so that we can encourage each other!

Love from Mary and Bob Bain

Email: marybain1@hotmail.co.uk

APPENDIX
TAMAR BY THE WAYSIDE

In chapter twelve, one of the prophetic words and pictures describes Tamar sitting by the wayside:-

'I saw <u>Tamar, sitting by a roadside,</u> and a righteous resolution and restoration of proper relationships in the house. No longer would her gifting be left in limbo, abused and out of place. Her father-in-law had left her hanging (see Genesis 38) but there will be resolution. The fig tree has been 'digged and dunged' and fruit is expected. Leave it for a year and the baby will be born. (Luke 13:8)'.

The following, hopefully, will give some background which will help unpack what this picture might mean to you. Our understanding of the parable of the fig tree, in Luke chapter thirteen, is that it would be cut down, if it didn't become fruitful. In the story of Tamar, in Genesis chapter thirty-eight, her father-in law, Judah, through God's grace, changes his ways, and repositions his household in to a place of blessing instead of destruction. Tamar's actions led to a righteous resolution.

Genesis chapter thirty-eight is one of the most 'censored' passages in the Bible. No-one talks about it much. It is the story of Tamar, a used and abused widow who God looks out for. Through her persistence, she secures her future in spite of the ungodly and unjust mess she finds herself in, and goes on a journey of faith with the people of God.

SHE DIDN'T CHOOSE HER CIRCUMSTANCES.

She was married into a mess.
There were hidden family secrets going on. Judah had left Jacob and his brothers, and was numbing his conscience in Canaan and its culture. He was the one who had suggested selling his brother, Joseph into slavery because they were all jealous of him. This had set off his father, Jacob, into a grieving process for a dead son, who in reality hadn't been killed at all. The grieving had gone on and on. She had been married in succession to Judah's sons, Er and Onan, both a bad lot. They are so wicked in their behaviour that God puts

both Er, and then Onan, to death. Judah, instead of recognising that their wickedness had been their downfall, blamed the widow, Tamar. He was nervous about his final son, Shelah's future. If Judah was to fulfill the Levirate custom, he would have to offer Shelah to Tamar in marriage. But then, perhaps Shelah would end up being the next one to die, if he married her.

HER FUTURE WAS BEING SHUT DOWN

Tamar had the legal customs about widows and inheritance on her side, but instead she was sent off back to her father, and left in a wedding-in-waiting limbo. She was neither being released by Judah to be free to move on, nor was she being given a secure future as a married woman within Judah's family. But it is clear, from the story, that her circumstances had come about by God's direct intervention. Er was a bad lot, and so God had killed him! Onan had been using her for casual sex, and hadn't taken his responsibility to continue the family line of his deceased brother seriously. So he too had died.

She was no longer properly her father's responsibility, yet she was back in her childhood home. The proper framework for her future security was elsewhere, in being married once more into her dead husband's family, and having children who would look after her in her older years. Judah was legally responsible to set her up properly but wasn't doing anything about it. When the youngest son, Shelah reached manhood, nothing changed. She knew then that Judah was never going to do the right thing, but intended to shut her out of her future. She was by now probably in her late twenties and the future looked bleak. There were plenty of opportunities to be bitter. She knew the kind of man Judah was, and everything looked hopeless.

DESPERATE BUT DETERMINED.

However, Tamar persisted, and didn't give up. She hit on a life or death plan to come through into a new place of peace. Like the story Jesus told of the widow with her petition to the unjust judge, she also persisted (Lk 18:1-8). The unjust judge, in the story, eventually dealt with her case, motivated by his sinful desire to get her off his back, so he could get back to life as usual. His behaviour was appalling but brought about a righteous outcome. In his office as judge he eventually did the right thing.

Tamar really did know the man! Judah was, by now, himself widowed, and probably about fifty. She knew that, if she could set herself up to look like a shrine prostitute, when Judah came by, his poor sexual behaviour would give her the chance she needed. Behind the veil, sitting by the roadside, she wasn't recognised, and Judah slept with her. Afterwards, she made sure that he left her a security pledge to pay later, and so he unwittingly provided her with the proof she needed that he had slept with her. As a pledge, he gave her his signet, his cord and his staff.

GOD FAVOURS HER

The Levirate obligation to provide for the widow was about to be fulfilled. From that one encounter with Judah, she actually conceived, and three months later it was obvious to everyone. She was answerable to Judah for her behaviour. You can almost hear his glee at being able to solve his problem, and get Tamar executed. He would be the one passing judgment. The penalty for her immorality as a woman, under obligation to marry his son, Shelah, would be death by burning. But on the way to him, she sent him the message discreetly, about who had got her pregnant, and Judah's conscience convicted him of his unjust behaviour towards her – he had denied her children from within his family line. He concludes that 'She is more righteous than I', and having fulfilled his physical duty unwittingly, he doesn't sleep with her again. Twins are born - Perez and Zerah. Tamar's wedding limbo is resolved, with a righteous outcome. As it turns out, one of the twins, Perez is in the direct line of the family tree of Jesus (and means 'breakthrough'!).

SHE WAS INCLUDED IN THE PROMISES OF GOD

We can argue that she wanted to be a part of whatever it was that this family had. She will have heard of the special relationship this family claimed it had with God, the stories of God's dealings with Abraham, Isaac and then Jacob. It came with all the family mess, but it also came with the promises of God.

She got in on God's blessing and provision for her life. Perez and Zerah grew up and had children. They are all listed, along with Judah, in the seventy that later joined Joseph in Egypt to escape the famine. By then, Judah would have been in his seventies, and unless she died young, Tamar, now in her fifties, would have been there too.

Unwittingly and wickedly, Judah, in choosing to sell his brother, Joseph, rather than kill him, had brought about the rescue of himself and his whole family, and the opportunity for family reconciliation. By then, Judah was a very different man, willing to lay down his life to spare his father any further grief. This change in behaviour had really begun through Tamar. She had persisted, not accepting the limbo that Judah had put her in, and finally she was able to take her proper position in the family.

GOD LOVES OUTSIDERS

Matthew's gospel list of the family tree of Jesus has four women included in it who are all outside gentiles with dubious backgrounds. God had included them all.

God loves outsiders. There are people that God wants to include, who He has called into His family, and who carry tremendous blessing with them. Instead of being embraced, and properly positioned where they can be fruitful, they are often used and abused, and left in limbo. Their contribution to the church is rejected by the ones who should have received them. God sees the Tamars sitting by the wayside, and comes to their rescue.

BOOKS FROM OPEN WELLS PUBLISHING

BY THE SAME AUTHORS

Becoming Multi-flavoured Church

Singing over Havering

Prayer Walking around Redbridge

Launching after Lockdown

Poems:

My Song Matters

Beyond the Door

Available from www.lulu.com or Amazon

Media: A fifty minute film –

youtube search for

"God on the Move – Havering"

Welcome Network youtube channel

Bob and Mary Bain at Alnmouth, Northumberland.

To God be the glory!

Printed in Poland
by Amazon Fulfillment
Poland Sp. z o.o., Wrocław

59800291R00076